MW00526532

Inside Passage
Walking Tours

Inside Passage Walking Tours

Exploring Ketchikan, Juneau, Skagway & Sitka

Julianne Chase Patton

Writer & Co. Publishing

Library of Congress Control Number: 2011924110

ISBN 978-0-615-45140-4
1. Travel   2. Alaska

Writer & Co. Publishing
P.O. Box 2914
Bremerton, WA 98310

Contents

Introduction

The fabled Inside Passage threads its way through Southeast Alaska, a spectacularly beautiful land of islands, rain forests, soaring mist-layered mountains and abundant wildlife from both land and sea. Some 10,000 years ago massive glaciers of the last ice age sculpted this land, carving the fjords and creating the thousand or so islands that make up the Alexander Archipelago.

Each of the picturesque coastal towns along the Inside Passage has its own flavor: totem poles and fishing boats in Ketchikan; state government and mining in Juneau; the Klondike Gold Rush, alive and well in Skagway; and echoes of Russian America in Sitka.

Southeast Alaska also is home to some of the state's first peoples: the Tlingit, Haida and Tsimshian, whose rich heritage is celebrated in lofty totem poles and beautiful beadwork, basketry and other artworks.

As different as they are from one another, the towns of the Inside Passage share many similarities. The wilderness is only steps away from the concrete of the city streets and the casual outdoor-oriented lifestyle is woven into the fabric of the place. There's a sense of freedom here, reflected in the spirit and independence of the people who call it home. Individuals count here and they have a "can-do" attitude that ensures that they will indeed make a difference. It's still a place where you can be on a first-name basis with your congressional representative or governor.

This book and its walking tours introduce you to the towns of Ketchikan, Juneau, Skagway and Sitka. You'll find out how they came to be and what it's like to live there, as well as some of the things about them both wonderful and a little weird. All of the walking tours are circular routes; you can start anywhere and return to that point. The stops are numbered on a map to refer to when you want to visit, or return to, a specific spot.

Southeast's maritime climate is cool and often damp. Those who live here both ignore it and give it healthy respect. Plan for the layered look and wear comfortable low-heeled shoes. Sometimes it's warm and sunny, but when it's not, wear an extra sweater, pull on your rain gear and waterproof boots or shoes, and blend in with the locals. Most of all, enjoy your time here, whether it's for a day or a year.

A WORD ABOUT THE WILDERNESS

Each section of this book includes one or two day hikes that are the most accessible to the town. The following cautionary notes apply to hiking anywhere in Southeast Alaska:

- Tell someone where you are going and when you plan to return.
- Carry your own water and snacks, and make sure to pack out your trash.
- Wear your "Southeast sneakers" (rubber boots), waterproof shoes or boots and stay on the trail.
- Keep an eye out for bears. Most of the islands of Southeast have black bears in residence, but there are brown bears on the mainland and the "ABC islands": Admiralty, Baranof and Chichagof Islands (Sitka is on Baranof). If you see a bear, do not approach it or try to feed it. Never get between a mother and her cub. Bears usually prefer to avoid people, so make noise as you go along so you don't surprise one: sing to yourself, talk to others or jingle "bear bells." National Park and Forest Service offices have more information about bears.

At right: "Thundering Wings" totem in Eagle Park.

Ketchikan

Ketchikan At A Glance

Population:
Ketchikan Gateway Borough: 12,993 (19.1% Alaska Natives),
City of Ketchikan: 7,508 51.09% Men, 48.91% Women;
Visitors: 850,000 annually

Geography:
Ketchikan Gateway Borough: 4,898.9 sq. mi. of land; 1,981.3 sq. mi. of water.
City of Ketchikan: 3.4 sq. mi. of land, plus 0.8 sq. mi. of water.
Location: SW coast of Revillagigedo Island, fronting Tongass Narrows; 235 miles north to Juneau; 679 miles south to Seattle

Weather:
Average summer temperatures: 51-65° F
Average winter temperatures: 29-39° F
Annual precipitation: 162" (13.5'), including 32" of snow

Primary Industries:
Tourism (425 cruise ship calls annually), fishing (292 residents hold commercial fishing permits), fish-processing facilities and fish hatchery, wood products industry, government (2/3 of the state ferry system workers live in Ketchikan)

Facilities and Services:
A University of Alaska Southeast campus; full-service Ketchikan General Hospital. Newspapers: Ketchikan Daily News. Radio: KTKN 930-AM; KRBD (Rain Bird) 105.3-FM; KGTW 106.7-FM; KFMJ 99.9-FM. TV: cable television.

Visitor Information:
Ketchikan Visitors Bureau, 131 Front St., Ketchikan, AK 99901; 907-225-6166 or 800-770-3300.
Web site: http://www.visit-ketchikan.com;
E-mail: info@visit-ketchikan.com
Information on what to see and do in Ketchikan.

Southeast Alaska Discovery Center, 50 Main St., 907-228-6220. Web site: http://alaskacenters.gov/ketchkan.cfm
Information on Tongass National Forest, Misty Fiords National Park and other federal agencies.

Ketchikan

Ketchikan visitor to small boy on the dock:
"Has it been raining long?"
Small boy: "I don't know. I'm only five years old."

"Salmon Capital of the World." It's a big boast, but salmon are Ketchikan's reason for being. Before European explorers came on the scene, generations of Tongass and Cape Fox Tlingits had fish camps on Ketchikan Creek. They gave the place its name: "kitsch-khin," which means "thundering wings of an eagle."

American settlers came to the area in the 1880s, building a salmon saltery at the mouth of Ketchikan Creek. The first cannery opened in 1886; by 1936, Ketchikan was one of the largest exporters of salmon in the world, producing 1.5 million cases of salmon annually.

The need for lumber to build new businesses and homes, as well as packing boxes for the canneries, spawned the Ketchikan Spruce Mills in 1903. Ketchikan became a supply center for area logging; a pulp mill built at Ward Cove in 1954 helped fuel area growth. (The mill closed in 1997 and the city is seeking new economic development and ventures.)

Inside Passage Walking Tours

Today, fishing and tourism power the economy of Ketchikan, which has grown to be Alaska's fourth largest city. In the process, it has earned a couple of additional nicknames: "Alaska's First City," because it's the first city in Alaska that northbound ferries and cruise ships reach, and, more recently, "Totem Town," because

of all the totem poles – at least 113 – scattered in various locations around the Ketchikan area. The totems, along with colorful Creek Street

Creek Street is "where fishermen and salmon went upstream to spawn."

(a reminder of an earlier, bawdier time), are major draws for visitors.

Even though the body of water in front of town might look like a river, it's not. That saltwater channel is Tongass Narrows. Across the way are Gravina Island and the smaller Pennock Island. Ketchikan itself is on an island: Revillagigedo (ruh-VEE-ah-hey-

hey-doe). It was named by Spaniards for the 18th-century viceroy of New Spain (Mexico) who supported the Spanish exploration of Alaska. Instead of trying to pronounce this tongue-twister, just say "Revilla" (ruh-VIL-ah) like the locals do.

Much of downtown Ketchikan was built on pilings. Many buildings are original structures and often have trapdoors that were once used by bootleggers. Boardwalks and trestle streets were common in earlier times, and although most have been replaced or paved over, a few can still be seen (Stops #7 and #14 on the walking tour).

Visitors are fascinated to discover that what may appear to be a street on a map is actually a flight of wooden stairs, often the only access to homes on the steep slopes. Residents sometimes hire helicopters to move heavy furniture in or out of their hillside homes. And, you'd certainly think twice before buying something large and bulky if it had to be hauled up 100 or so stairs.

Downtown Ketchikan is so compact that visitors can go exploring without worrying about losing their way. You can't get far. Only 18.4 miles north and 12.9 miles south, the roads stop. And we're not kidding: The signs literally say "Road Ends." There's also not much crime to speak of, although there was a bank robbery a while back. Seems a 19-year-old kid with bad judgment robbed First Bank and then raced around the corner – straight into the arms of the police, who were running down Main from the station to answer the bank's silent alarm.

Ketchikan's topography and geology have resulted in some peculiarities. Because of the very thin topsoil, gravesites at Bayview Cemetery are periodically blasted out of the rock and then soil is hauled in. The town was built literally up the sides of the hills, with some homes at the 100-foot elevation level.

"Ketchikan is 5 miles long, 7 blocks wide and 5 inches deep."

Residents make use of every square inch of their property, often adding on a room here and there as the need arises. And, being an independent lot, they tend not to take no for an answer – even, or maybe especially, from the city fathers. There's a local story about a homeowner who, refused permission to tear down a house and rebuild on his too-small lot, constructed new walls and a roof around the outside of the old house, and then tore it down from the inside out. "You could see the old walls right through the windows of the new one," remembered one local.

Ketchikan is blessed with about 160 inches (more than 13 feet) of precipitation annually – most of it rain. A sunny day is something to celebrate with a spontaneous picnic or fishing trip. However, you might see a few locals walking around looking a little "sun-shocked," with hats pulled low to shade their eyes. Residents take the rain in stride. They go fishing in the rain. They play sports in the rain. Baseball and soccer games are almost never called on account of rain; they'd never make it through the season otherwise. (Basketball, not surprisingly, is extremely popular throughout Southeast Alaska.)

"If you can't see the top of Deer Mountain, it's raining. If you can, it's going to rain."

The Tongass National Forest and its array of recreational opportunities is Ketchikan's backyard, but living next to the great outdoors does have its hazards. The best bear viewing used to be at the dump, but the city has controlled them there, so now the bears have branched out and can be seen occasionally meandering through the streets. Bald eagles have been known to snatch up a small dog or a cat. And a pack of wolves once chased a person up a tree in an outlying area.

It's easier for women to get a date in Ketchikan: 51.09% of residents are male, 48.91% female.

FESTIVALS AND OTHER FUN

Among the special events unique to Ketchikan are: Festival of the North in February, a month-long celebration of music and theatrical productions, visual and literary arts, including the Wearable Art and Quilting in the Rain shows; Hummingbird Festival in April celebrating the return of the Rufous Hummingbird with birding events and an art show; King Salmon Derby on Memorial Day weekend and the first two weekends in June, with more than $10,000 in prizes for big fish; the original melodrama "Fish Pirate's Daughter" in July; the Blueberry Arts Festival in August featuring a slug race; and the Winter Art Faire in November. Check out the *Ketchikan Daily News* for what's going on when you're there.

DON'T MISS

Any visitor to Ketchikan shouldn't miss:

- The Totem Heritage Center (Stop #12 on the walking tour), with the nation's largest collection of nineteenth-century totem poles
- The Southeast Alaska Visitor Center (Stop #2), with its excellent exhibits on Native American culture, Southeast Alaska's ecosystems and resources, and the rain forest
- A visit to Creek Street, with its shops and restaurants (Stops #17-20)
- A ride on the Cape Fox funicular (Stop #19) for the spectacular view

Inside Passage Walking Tours

At left, clockwise from top left: 1904 Burkhart-Dibrell House; Dolly's House museum on Creek Street; waterfront promenade; Native American artist's shop on Creek Street. Above: Cape Fox funicular.

Inside Passage Walking Tours

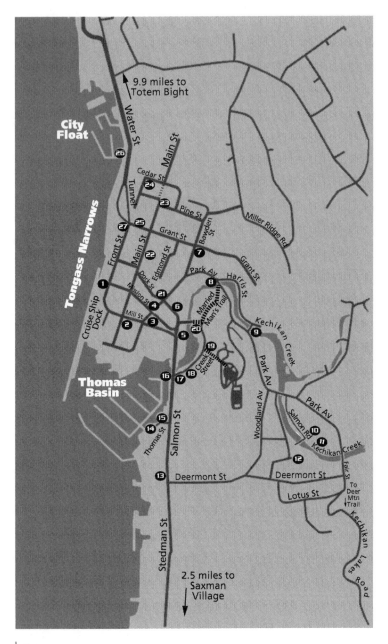

9.9 miles to Totem Bight

City Float

Water St

Main St

Cedar St

Tunnel

Pine St

Bawden St

Miller Ridge Rd

Grant St

Front St

Mill St

Grant St

Tongass Narrows

Mission St

Dock St

Edmond St

Park Av

Harris St

Married Man's Trail

Kechikan Creek

Cruise Ship Dock

Park Av

Creek Street

Park Av

Thomas Basin

Woodland Av

Salmon Rd

Kechikan Creek

Salmon St

Thomas St

Fair St

Deermont St

Deermont St

Lotus St

To Deer Mtn Trail

Kechikan Lakes Road

Stedman St

2.5 miles to Saxman Village

The Walking Tour

Inside Passage Walking Tours

Ketchikan Walking Tour

This walking tour through Ketchikan's central downtown features historic buildings, totem poles, a fish hatchery, shopping on Creek Street and scenic viewpoints. The terrain is mostly flat, although a few steep hills are on the route, along with some optional stair climbs with the reward of a scenic view from the top. Estimated time: 2-2 ½ hours – longer if you linger to shop or savor the views. (Note: Numbered walking tour signs you will encounter refer to the Ketchikan Visitors Bureau's tour. This tour visits all of those stops – and more – but not necessarily in the same order.)

1 Start the tour on the cruise ship dock at the **Ketchikan Visitors Bureau Information Center**, 131 Front Street, THE source of information on local sightseeing and visitor facilities. Outside, look for the Ketchikan Rain Gauge, with tongue-in-cheek information about local weather history. 🚻 ♿

Across from the visitor's center is Mission Street, part of Ketchikan's main downtown shopping area. The Welcome Arch replicates previous arches dating back to the 1920s, when the first one was erected to greet steamship passengers.

From the front door of the Visitors Bureau, turn right on Front Street, which curves to become Mill Street. Continue along Mill Street for a block to Main Street.

At the end of Main Street is the **Great Alaskan Lumberjack Show**, 420 Spruce Mill Way, featuring events like buck sawing, axe throwing, power sawing, logrolling and a 50-foot pole climb. Covered grandstand. Shows daily May-Sept. Adult admission $29; children $14.50. Advance tickets recommended. For information, call 907-225-9050 or toll-free 1-888-320-9049.

Stop to Shop The two main areas for boutiques and galleries are downtown across from the cruise ship dock and Creek Street. (In the summer, some shops may be closed when there are no ships in port.) A few suggested places to stop and shop are:

SCANLON GALLERY, 318 Mission St. Works by major Alaskan artists and locals as well as traditional and contemporary Alaska Native artwork.

SALMON, ETC., 322 Mission St. With Ketchikan calling itself the "Salmon Capital of the World," it wouldn't do to leave without some, whether it's smoked, canned or frozen.

Creek Street has numerous great shops. The Star Building at 5 Creek Street has three in particular that are well worth visiting:

PARNASSUS (upstairs). A local bookstore carrying an eclectic assortment of new, old, and Alaska books; classical and jazz music; and distinctive gifts.

THE SOHO COHO (boardwalk level). Featuring the droll, wearable fish-themed artwork of Ketchikan's own Ray Troll: "The DaVinci Cod", "Blues in the Key of Sea," and more.

ALASKA EAGLE ARTS (boardwalk level). A fine art gallery featuring Pacific Northwest Native artworks.

Also at the foot of Main is the **Alaska Fish House**, 3 Salmon Landing. ⅄ ALASKA FISH HOUSE.

⋀⋀ *Cross Main Street.*

❷ To the right is the **Southeast Alaska Discovery Center**, 50 Main Street, one of four Alaska Public Lands Information Centers, offering information about the Tongass National Forest, plus other federal agencies.

The center has several totem poles and excellent dioramas on Native American culture: salmon fishing, wood carving, food preservation and preparation. Other exhibits explore Southeast Alaska's ecosystems and resources. Audiovisual presentations accompany the exhibits. In the Native American exhibit, elders tell tales of traditional life. You'll hear bird calls and waves in the ecosystems exhibit, while the resources exhibit features narrations about commercial fishing, mining, recreation and the wilderness.

There's a theater, trip planning room and bookstore. Reservations for Forest Service cabins can be made here. May-Sept. open Mon.-Sat., 8 a.m.-5 p.m.; Sun. 8 a.m.-4 p.m. Admission $5. Oct.-April open Tues.-Sat. 10 a.m.-4:30 p.m. with free admission. 🎭 ♿

⋀⋀ *From the Discovery Center, turn right along Mill Street and go half a block to Bawden Street. Cross Mill Street to the park.*

❸ Sit on a bench and admire the flowers at **Whale Park** (named for its shape). The Knox Brothers Clock is Ketchikan's oldest public

Grabbing a Bite Following are a few suggested dining spots in Ketchikan. The number indicates where to look for them as you follow the walking tour.

ALASKA FISH HOUSE, 3 Salmon Landing (at the foot of Main Street). (Stop #2). Serving sustainably-caught, wild Alaskan seafood. Mid-April to mid-Oct. Mon.-Fri: 9 a.m.-4 p.m.; Sat.-Sun: 9:30 a.m.-2:30 p.m. Phone: 907-247-4057. $$

PIONEER CAFÉ, 619 Mission Street. (Stop #4). Rub shoulders with the locals at this self-described "friendliest place in town." Specialties include Alaskan seafood and reindeer sausage. Open 24 hours; non-smoking. Breakfast, lunch, dinner. $-$$

THE NEW YORK HOTEL & CAFÉ, 207 Stedman St. (Stop #16) Offering a variety of sandwiches and soup, plus espresso drinks from their own Ketchikan Coffee Company. Deck overlooks Ketchikan Creek. Breakfast, lunch. Phone: 907-225-0246 $-$$

HEEN KAHIDI RESTAURANT, Cape Fox Hotel, 800 Venetia Way (Stop #19). Great views of Tongass Narrows. Specializes in seafood; varied menu from Belgian waffles to burgers to burnt cream. Full bar. Open 8 a.m.-10 p.m. Daily breakfast, lunch, dinner. Phone: 907-225-8001 $$-$$$

ANNABELLE'S RESTAURANT, 326 Front St., in the Gilmore Hotel. (Stop #27). Features "Alaska hospitality in elegant surroundings" with a 1920s atmosphere. Full bar. Daily lunch, dinner. Phone: 907-225-6009 $$-$$$

timepiece. The Chief Kyan totem pole, by master carver Israel Shotridge, was erected in 1993 as a replica of the original raised in the 1890s for the chief, whose fish camp was nearby. The crane on top represents Chief Kyan's wife. Just below is the Thunderbird, symbol of his wife's clan. At the bottom is the Bear crest of the chief. 📷

🚶 From the park, continue right on Bawden to the next corner.

4 At Mission and Bawden Streets is **St. John's Episcopal Church and Seamen's Center**, 423 Mission St. Ketchikan's oldest church, St. John's was built in 1903. Like many older build-

ings downtown, it was built on pilings and seawater routinely rises in the basement during extremely high tides. The Seamen's Center, serving those who make their living on and from the sea, was constructed in 1904 as a hospital.

There's a Post Office substation across the street at 422 Mission St. ✉

🚶 From St. John's, turn right on Mission Street, passing along Whale Park, to Dock Street and cross over.

On the way is the **Pioneer Café, 619 Mission Street.** 🍴 PIONEER CAFÉ.

5 The **Chief Johnson Totem Pole**, belonging to the Kadjuk House of the Raven Clan of the Tlingit tribe, is a replica carved by Israel Shotridge and raised in 1989. The original, erected in 1901 by Chief Johnson himself, can be seen at the Totem Heritage Center.

⚇ *Proceed left on Dock Street half a block.*

⑥ The Centennial Building, 629 Dock Street, houses the **Tongass Historical Museum and Public Library**. The library has an extensive Alaskan collection and is a state document repository.

The museum has a very good exhibit on Tlingit, Tsimshian and Haida cultures developed through consultations with Native elders. Other exhibits include Ketchikan's history as the "Salmon Capital of the World," a c.1901 fire department hand pumper, early-day curios and a case of trade beads collected in the 1940s and '50s.

May-Sept., open daily, 8 a.m.-5 p.m.; Oct.-April, open 1-5 p.m. Tues.-Fri., 10 a.m.-4 p.m. Sat. Admission charged May-Sept. only: adults $2; children 12 and under, free.

Next to the museum is the **"Raven Stealing the Sun" totem pole** by Dempsey Bob, raised in 1983. An overlook to Ketchikan Creek offers a view of spawning salmon during the summer and a creek side wooden sculpture of a giant king salmon created by Haida master carver Jones Yeltatzie in honor of the 1967 centennial of Alaska's purchase from Russia.

⚇ *From the museum, head right on Dock Street half a block, turn right on Bawden Street for one block, then turn right on Park Avenue.*

OPTION: For a shorter tour, featuring the shopping areas of Creek Street and downtown, but skipping the Salmon Ladder, Deer Mountain Fish Hatchery, and the Totem Heritage Center:

🚶🚶 *Retrace your steps from the museum through the parking lot to the entrance of Creek Street (Stop #21), the funicular (Stop #20), and out to Stedman (Stop #17). Turn right on Stedman Street, which will take you back to the cruise ship pier and the downtown shopping area.*

❼ Straight ahead as you walk up Bawden Street, you can see the **Grant Street Trestle**. On the National Register of Historic Places, this is Ketchikan's last wood trestle. In the city's early years, all of the sidewalks and streets were built as trestles, so residents could easily negotiate the steep slopes.

Nearby historic homes on the National Register are the c.1900 **Ziegler House**, 623 Grant St., and the 1920 **Walker-Broderick House**, 541 Pine St., just a block up the hill from the trestle.

🚶🚶 *Proceed along the right-hand side of Park Avenue for 3-5 minutes.*

You'll pass the **American Legion Post #3**, 631 Park Ave. The post was established in 1919; the building dates to 1932.

🚶 *Look for a sign on the fence with an arrow pointing the way to the Salmon Ladder. Turn right and follow the boardwalk to a wooden observation deck.*

The Legend of How Raven Stole the Sun

A traditional Southeast Alaska Native legend tells how Raven brought light to the world. In Ketchikan, visitors will find the story depicted in the totem pole "Raven Stealing the Sun," located next to the museum on Dock Street.

As the legend goes, Raven desired the Sun, Moon and Stars, which were owned by a powerful chief.

So, Raven changed himself into a spruce needle and fell into a stream. The spruce needle was swallowed by the old chief's daughter as she drank from the stream. She became pregnant and gave birth to a son who was really Raven, the trickster.

The old man loved his grandson and gave him anything he wanted. The child cried and begged for the containers of light and eventually the old chief relented and gave the boxes to the boy.

One by one, Raven opened the boxes, releasing the Sun, the Moon and the Stars through the lodge's smoke hole. And so it came to pass that Raven brought light to the world.

8 The concrete **Salmon Ladder** enables salmon returning from the sea to bypass the falls so they can reach the upper stretches of Ketchikan Creek to spawn. From the deck, watch migrating salmon during the summer.

Retrace your steps to Park Avenue and continue to the right. Cross the street and walk along Ketchikan Creek for about 10 minutes.

OPTION: For a shorter tour, bypassing the salmon hatchery and Totem Heritage Center and proceeding to the Creek Street shops, look for the sign for the Married Man's Trail on Park Avenue, just as you cross the creek. The trail meanders off to the right for a 2-3 minute walk to Creek Street. Married Man's Trail was so-named because men from the town took this trail through the woods, particularly during Prohibition, to visit the Creek Street bawdy houses to get a drink, play cards or visit the "sporting women."

As a second option, take the upper portion of the trail-up four flights of stairs (65 steps) and then a trail through the woods with peek-a-boo views of the town. It's 10-15 minutes to the Cape Fox Hotel. Take the funicular tram down to Creek Street from the hotel lobby.

9 **Park Avenue** passes through a residential area. There are good views of spawning salmon during the summer and fishermen, particularly from the Harris Street Bridge. (A note to birdwatchers: Just past Harris Street is Freeman Street, a short dead end. Along the creek across from Freeman is a sandhill crane nesting area. Among the tallest birds in the world, with wingspans of six to seven feet, these birds may be seen throughout Southeast Alaska in the spring and fall.)

Inside Passage Walking Tours

🚶 Park Avenue curves and then crosses a bridge. Just after the bridge, cross the street and head to the right on Salmon Road to the fish hatchery.

🔟 Deer Mountain Tribal Hatchery & Eagle Center, a subsidiary of the Ketchikan Indian Corp., was built in 1954. Each year it raises and releases some 300,000 baby salmon (smolts). Since 1998, the Eagle Center has rehabilitated bald eagles and other raptors for display and educational programs.

Interpretive displays depict the life cycle of salmon and visitors can watch hatchery operations. The Tribal Gift Shop supports the hatchery by selling Native arts and crafts, smoked and canned salmon, salmon-skin leather accessories, books and souvenirs.

Open 8 a.m.-4:30 p.m. daily, late April to mid-Sept. Guided tours available. Admission: $10 for adults; military, $5; children 2-11, $5; children under 2, free. 🚻 ♿

🚶 Follow the path around the side of the hatchery and along the creek for about a minute to City Park.

⓫ City Park has tree-shaded picnic areas near small ponds originally constructed in the early 1900s as part of the city's first fish hatchery. Volunteers restored the park's fountain in 1989. 🚻 ♿

🚶 Just inside the park, turn right over a stone footbridge, and walk for 1-2 minutes.

⓬ The Totem Heritage Center, a National Historic Landmark, houses the nation's largest collection of historic totem poles, with some up to 150 years old. The City of Ketchikan built the center in 1976 to preserve and display 33 original totem poles, house posts and pole fragments from 19th century Tlingit villages on Tongass and Village islands and from the Haida village of Old Kasaan. All are within 50 miles of Ketchikan and were abandoned as residents moved away for jobs and schooling.

Exhibits include contemporary Tlingit, Haida and Tsimshian ceremonial clothing and beadwork and an exhibit of Chilkat weaving. The center offers a nationally-recognized program of Native arts classes; the gift shop sells Native artwork. Information about indigenous plants is posted along a nature trail. There are special exhibits for the sight-impaired.

Open 8 a.m.-5 p.m. daily, May 1-Sept. 30; 1-5 p.m. Mon.-Fri., Oct. 1-April 30. Admission May 1-Sept. 30 is $5 for adults; children 12 and under free. 📖 ♿

From the front of the Totem Heritage Center, go left to Deermont Street, then turn right down the hill 10-12 minutes to Stedman Street.

As you walk down Deermont, you'll pass by St. **Elizabeth's Church**, used for worship from 1927-1962 and now a mortuary. Further down the hill, on the right is the **Ketchikan Indian Community** office building, featuring eagle and raven panels created by Tlingit artist Ernie Smeltzer and high school students in 1983.

Turn right on Stedman Street.

13 Across Stedman Street, you'll see the University of Alaska Southeast's Robertson Building. In front stands the **Sun Raven totem pole**, created by master carver Israel Shotridge in 2003 as a replica of one that stood in the early 1900s at Tongass Island, the ancestral home of the Tongass Tribe of Tlingit Indians.

Continue to the right along Stedman Street for 4-5 minutes.

Across Stedman Street, you'll see a totem pole at a private residence. Depicting three watchmen, an eagle, raven and a man with a talking stick, it was carved by Haida artist Warren Peele.

Cross Stedman Street and turn left on Thomas Street.

14 Thomas Street, one of the few remaining wooden streets in Ketchikan, originally provided access to the former New England Fish Company cannery. Entering the street, you'll pass 158 Thomas Street, built in 1912 and part of the **Thomas Street Historic District.**

A variety of maritime- and commercial fishing-related businesses are in the area, including the Potlatch Bar, 126 Thomas Street, known as "the fishermen's bar."

Near the end of the street, which narrows to a sidewalk, look over the side and you'll see grids of heavy timbers that support boats so their hulls can be painted or repaired at low tide.

Continue on the **waterfront promenade** out along the breakwater, which affords excellent views of the fishing fleet, cruise ship dock, downtown area, Tongass Narrows and Deer Mountain. 📷

Retrace your steps on Thomas Street and turn left to the Thomas Street Viewing Platform.

15 **The Thomas Street Viewing Platform** is a great place to photograph the fishing boats and pleasure craft in Thomas Basin. A kiosk has a display about the fishing industry and its role in Ketchikan's history and economy. Wood benches and tables make lingering a pleasure.

🚶 Continue along the viewing platform and boardwalk back to Stedman Street, turn left and walk to the bridge.

16 From the **Stedman Street Bridge**, spanning the mouth of Ketchikan Creek, you can watch salmon heading upstream to spawn, and fishermen young and old trying to catch them. Ketchikan Creek produces four of the five species of salmon, including king (chinook) from June to mid-August; coho (silver) from September through October; and pink (humpy) and chum (dog) from mid-July through August. From late fall through May, the big fish in the creek are steelhead trout.

Across the street is the **New York Hotel & Café**, 207 Stedman St. 🍴 THE NEW YORK HOTEL & CAFÉ

🚶 Cross Stedman to the entrance of Creek Street and the viewing platform.

17 **Creek Street** was Ketchikan's red light district from 1903-53. During its heyday, the board street had more than 30 houses of ill repute, most with one or two "sporting women." Bootleggers operated here during Prohibition, passing liquor up through trapdoors during high tides at night.

Today, this is a major shopping area, with most of the houses converted to shops or restaurants, although a few remain private

Creek Street's Colorful Legacy

Colorful Creek Street (Stops #17-20) is "where fishermen and salmon went upstream to spawn."

A plank street built on pilings over Ketchikan Creek, the street began its notorious era as Ketchikan's official red light district in 1903, when the City Council banished all bawdy houses south of Ketchikan Creek to Creek Street and south Stedman.

During its heyday, more than 30 houses on Creek Street were operated by "sporting women," as they preferred to call themselves. Because a Territorial law defined a house of prostitution as a place inhabited by more than two "female boarders" (a euphemism for prostitutes), most Creek Street houses were occupied by only one or two women, who went by such fanciful names as Frenchy, Black Mary and Dirty Neck Maxine.

Before, during and after Prohibition, these sporting gals also ran speakeasies, supplied by bootleggers operating from the Canadian port of Prince Rupert, British Columbia, a convenient 90 miles south. Liquor was hoisted through trapdoors from the bootleggers' boats at high tide. The houses were shut down in 1953 after a grand jury investigation of several scandals, two of which involved the chief of police and a police captain (both were indicted and convicted).

The most famous of the Creek Street residents was Dolly Arthur, the "stage name" of one Thelma Copeland. Dolly's House is now a museum (Stop #18). Most of the other houses along picturesque Creek Street are now shops or restaurants; a few remain private residences.

residences. Creek Street is a Historic District; notable buildings include:

- #28 Creek Street, built in 1899;
- #24 Creek Street, c.1906, now a museum;
- #5 Creek Street, the Star Building, built in 1898 (the star in-laid in the hardwood floor is a legacy of the building's earlier life as a dance hall).

Continue along Creek Street a minute to #24, a light green house with red trim.

18 #24 Creek Street, built around 1906, is **Dolly's House**. Dolly Arthur was Ketchikan's most famous "sporting woman." The home where she lived from 1919 until 1973 is now a private museum. Self-guided tours are available when cruise ships are in port; there is an admission charge.

Visitors will see Dolly's own furniture and other belongings throughout the house, a secret cupboard for bootleg liquor, an interesting "facility" for gentlemen visitors, and more. Recordings in several rooms narrate Dolly's story.

From Dolly's continue along Creek Street's wind-ing boardwalk for 5 minutes (or more, depending on how much shopping you do). Toward the other end of Creek Street is the Cape Fox Hotel's funicular.

19 Near the entrance to the funicular, look around the corner to the left to see a tunnel approximately 10 feet deep in the rock face. This is a **Venetia Lode mine "adit"** (shaft) dug by miners in the 1890s to fulfill the requirement that they do some work every year to "prove up" their claim even though nothing much ever came of the mine work.

The Cape Fox funicular, a tram that operates like an eleva-tor, runs 130 feet up the side of Boston Smith Hill to the lobby of the Cape Fox Hotel. Sometimes there is a small charge to ride the funicular, but usually it is free. It shuts down at midnight.

The hotel, built and owned by the Cape Fox Indian Corporation, opened in 1990. From the top, enjoy a panoramic view of Tongass Narrows and the city below. Centerpiece of the lobby is the large cedar "Sun Raven" screen, by internationally renowned master carver Nathan  Jackson. The lobby library and second-floor balcony house a collection of Alaska Native artifacts. Outside the front entrance, you'll see a collection of six 10-foot totem poles by another acclaimed carver, Lee Wallace. "The Council of Clans" represents Tlingit clan figures of Saxman Village. 📷

Just off the hotel lobby is the **Heen Kahidi Restaurant**. ✕
HEEN KAHIDI RESTAURANT

Across the parking lot is the Ted Ferry Civic Center. 🏢 ♿

↳ Retrace your steps back through the Cape Fox lobby to the funicular and return to Creek Street. Follow the boardwalk toward the right to the footbridge.

🌑 **The footbridge across Ketchikan Creek** is a good spot to photograph Creek Street and to watch migrating salmon. A kiosk on the other side has historical information about Creek Street. 📷

↳ Continue through the parking lot to Dock Street. Proceed to the right for about a block and a half to the corner of Dock and Edmond Streets and turn right.

21 **The Ketchikan Daily News building** on the corner was built in 1925 as a U.S. Post Office. Take a moment to read the plaque on the side of the newspaper building before continuing to Edmond Street, named for Agnes Edmond, an Episcopal missionary who arrived in 1898 – the third white woman, and first single one, to live in Ketchikan.

You'll notice right away that **Edmond Street** isn't. A street, that is. Adapting to the terrain in true Ketchikan style, Edmond Street is a flight of 126 stairs, with nine landings on which to catch your breath. It's worth the climb. From the top, there's a great view of downtown Ketchikan, Deer Mountain, and Tongass Narrows. 📷

↟↟ *Retrace your steps to Dock Street and turn right for a block to Main Street, then turn right up the hill.*

ATMs are located at Wells Fargo Bank and First Bank, on opposite corners at the intersection of Dock and Main Streets. 💲

You'll pass the **Ketchikan Fire Department** on the left, then the office of the **Ketchikan Arts and Humanities Council** on the right, followed by the **Red Men Lodge**, Ketchikan's first fraternal organization, founded in 1900.

22 On the way up the Main Street hill, you'll cross **Grant Street**, named for early 20th century resident O.W. "Six-Shooter" Grant, who was always armed and rumored to sleep with his pistols. Across Grant from the police station, the large concrete edifice is the state office building.

↟↟ *At Grant, cross the street to continue up the hill to the intersection of Main and Pine Streets.*

23 Overlooking the Main Street stairs is the turreted **Burkhart-Dibrell House** (also called the Monrean House). On the National Register of Historic Places, the Queen Anne-style home was constructed in 1904 for H.Z. Burkhart, builder of Ketchikan's first sawmill.

OPTION: The Main Street Stairs offer another opportunity to take a climb – 120 steps to the top. There are good views of Tongass Narrows and downtown on the way up, but the view from the top is obscured by trees.

Continue left on Pine Street for one block and turn right to the Knob Hill Overlook.

24 A boardwalk extension of the street, the **Knob Hill Overlook** clings to the side of the hill, affording spectacular views and photo opportunities of Tongass Narrows, the busy waterfront, and Gravina and Pennock islands.

Most of the large homes in this Knob Hill area around Pine and Front Streets were built in the early 1900s for local merchants.

Retrace your steps back to Pine and go straight ahead to the Front Street Stairs, then down 116 steps. Good views of downtown and the waterfront. At the bottom, turn to the right through the tunnel (the street becomes Water Street on the other side of the tunnel).

Inside Passage Walking Tours

25 Drilling of the **Ketchikan Tunnel** through Knob Hill was completed in 1954. Prior to that, traffic went around the side of the hill on one-lane Water Street, alternating directions for a few minutes at a time. When a pulp mill was built at nearby Ward Cove, fueling the town's growth, another roadway was needed to accommodate the traffic. Since many of the city fathers lived atop Knob Hill and opposed blasting it to smithereens, the tunnel was the solution.

The 274-foot-long Ketchikan Tunnel is said to be the only one anywhere that you can drive over, around, and through.

At the other end of the tunnel, cross Water Street and proceed straight ahead to the Waterfront Promenade.

To the left on the promenade is a **Ketchikan Visitors Association** information center.

Proceed to the right half a block to a wooden deck park.

26 From **Harborview Park**, overlooking the City Float, you can see fishing boats, float planes, and marine traffic on Tongass Narrows. Decorated with hanging flower baskets in the summer, the park also has lots of wooden benches and picnic tables. A great spot to relax and watch the waterfront action.

OPTION: Stroll along the Waterfront Promenade for another 10-15 minutes to cruise ship berth #4 before returning to the downtown area.

From Harborview Park, turn right and head back on Water Street, this time around the outside of Knob Hill.

27 Rounding the hill, you'll come to **Eagle Park**. Its centerpiece is the "Thundering Wings" totem, carved by world-renowned Tlingit master carver Nathan Jackson.

Across the street is **Ketchikan City Hall** and **Annabelle's Restaurant**, 326 Front St.

Y ANNABELLE'S RESTAURANT

🚶 Cross the street and continue right on Front Street 2-3 minutes back to the cruise ship docks and the end of the walking tour.

What Time Is High Tide?

Ketchikan's elevation is sea level, although some of its neighborhoods rise to a scenic 100 feet.

If you've arrived by ship in the morning and come back in the afternoon, you will probably find either that the gangway enters the ship on a different deck or the gangway itself slopes at a greater or lesser degree than it did when you left. You're not imagining things. This is because (you may have noticed this) the ship floats. And, it floats up and down with the fluctuation of Ketchikan's 20 foot tides.

Tides are the alternate rise and fall of the earth's oceans, caused by the gravitational pull of the moon and the sun. Tides occur twice during each lunar day, which is 24 hours and 51 minutes, and which is why the tide is never high or low at the same time during our standard 24-hour day.

So, it's true that "time and tide wait for no man," but if you have a tide book (available at many locations, including drug and sporting goods stores), you can impress your friends by telling them when they can see the next high (or low) tide.

Inside Passage Walking Tours

Above, clockwise from top left: one of "The Council of Clans" totems at the Cape Fox Hotel; grid at Thomas Basin for repairing boats; Deer Mountain; totem pole at Southeast Alaska Discovery Center.

Getting Out of Town

TAKE A HIKE: DEER MOUNTAIN TRAIL

For a quick trip to the great outdoors, 3.25-mile Deer Mountain Trail is the closest to downtown Ketchikan. Deer Mountain is a 3,001-foot "horn," a pointy peak left after the glaciers receded 10,000 to 15,000 years ago.

To get to the trailhead from downtown, head south on Stedman Street and turn left on Deermont. Walk up the hill for 15 to 20 minutes to Fair Street, turn right and then follow the signs to the trail. (To save time, take a taxi to the trailhead.)

The well-used trail winds up the mountain through rain forest that quickly begins thinning out. It's relatively steep in places, with many switchbacks, so allow enough time (two to three hours to the summit) for a leisurely pace and to enjoy the views along the way. Overlooks at 1 mile and 2.5 miles; panoramic views of Ketchikan, Tongass Narrows and neighboring islands from the peak. The weather changes rapidly, so check the local forecast and be prepared. (Refer to page vii for general advice about hiking in Southeast Alaska.)

PLAY MISTY (FIORDS) FOR ME

Ketchikaners enjoy one of the biggest backyards in the world, the 16.9-million-acre Tongass National Forest.

All of Revillagigedo Island is in the national forest, which is the largest in the nation. Nearby (35 minutes by float plane) is dramatic 2.3-million-acre Misty Fiords National Monument, a rugged and scenic wilderness punctuated by vertical rock faces, plunging waterfalls and narrow waterways, accessible only by boat or float plane. Visitors can see ancient petroglyphs; mountain goats, deer or bear; and the 234-foot-tall volcanic core called New Eddystone Rock in East Behm Canal.

For an up-close wilderness experience, rent a Forest Service cabin for the bargain rate of $10-$65 a night. You'll get a fly-in or

The Lowdown on Ketchikan's Airport

Ketchikan has had an airport only since 1973. It had to be built across Tongass Narrows on Gravina Island – a short ferry ride away – because there was no flat land on Revillagigedo Island. It may be the only airport in the world that has its control tower situated lower than the runway – the runway is raised, so just the top of the tower sticks up past the runway level.

Before the airport opened, locals had to board the jets at the World War II-era, military-built airfield on Annette Island, 17 miles south of Ketchikan. They flew over to Annette via war-surplus PBYs (Catalinas), Grumman Goose and an assortment of other amphibious and pontoon-equipped aircraft.

hike-in cabin equipped with a stove for heating and cooking, an outhouse and wooden bunks (bring your own food, water, sleeping bags). Reserve a cabin at the U.S. Forest Service office in the Southeast Alaska Discovery Center, at 50 Main Street (Stop #2) or call 907-228-6220.

For a quicker, but equally sensational, visit to Misty Fiords, take a flightseeing excursion, which can be booked on board cruise ships or by calling, toll-free, Taquan Air, 800-770-8800; SeaWind Aviation, 877-225-1203; or Southeast Aviation, 888-359-6478. The Ketchikan Visitors Bureau on the downtown docks has information about other tours and operators.

TOTEM TOWN: SAXMAN NATIVE VILLAGE

The Ketchikan area has the largest Native American population of any municipality in the state; more than 19 percent of the population is Tsimshian, Tlingit or Haida, and their cultures flourish here. Saxman Native Village, 2.5 miles south of Ketchikan, fea-

Top left: Thomas Street viewing platform; celebratory totem located at Totem Heritage Center. Above: sculpture of king salmon alongside Ketchikan Creek.

tures one of the world's largest collection of totem poles (26 poles, some over 100 years old), a petroglyph rock, a traditional clan house, a production of Tlingit songs and dances by the Cape Fox Dancers, and master carvers and apprentices at work in the carving center. Local arts and crafts are available at the Village Store. Admission to the totem park and store is free.

Reach Saxman via a walking path along the South Tongass Highway (follow Stedman Street out of town and keep going); by taxi, city bus, or a tour available on board cruise ships or locally from Ketchikan Tours, 888-315-7881. The Saxman Village Store, 907-225-4421, also sells tour tickets.

TOTEM BIGHT STATE HISTORICAL PARK

Located 9.9 miles north of Ketchikan on North Tongass Highway, Totem Bight State Historical Park is a re-created Native village in a serene rain forest on a point overlooking Tongass Narrows. The park, on the National Register of Historic Places, was created in the 1930s as a Civilian Conservation Corps project under which skilled local carvers salvaged and re-created totem poles from abandoned villages that were in danger of destruction by the elements.

The park, reached by a short wooded path from a parking lot on the highway, has a replica of a clan house and 14 totems. Free admission; park open dawn to dusk year-round.

Totem Bight is easily accessible by car, taxi or city bus. It is also included in tours available on board cruise ships or Gray Line of Alaska, 800-544-2206. The Ketchikan Visitors Bureau has information about other tours and operators.

At right: "Windfall Fisherman" sculpture and Alaska's State Capitol.

Juneau

Juneau at a Glance

Population:
City and Borough of Juneau: 30,427 (16.6% Alaska Natives); 50.4% Men, 49.6% Women; Visitors: 790,000 annually

Geography:
City and Borough of Juneau: 2,716.7 sq. mi. of land; 538.3 sq. mi. of water.
Location: Mainland of Southeast Alaska panhandle, fronting Gastineau Channel; 577 air miles northwest to Anchorage, 900 air miles southeast to Seattle.

Weather:
Average summer temperatures: 44-65° F
Average winter temperatures: 25-35° F
Annual precipitation: 92" downtown, 54" just 10 miles north at the airport
Average annual snowfall: 101"
Tides: Range from 20.2 feet to -4.8 feet
Solstices: Summer (June 21): 18 hours, 18 minutes of daylight.
Winter (Dec. 21): 6 hours, 21 minutes of daylight.

Primary Industries:
Government (45% of all jobs), tourism (443 annual cruise ship calls), mining, including the largest silver mine in North America, support services for logging and fishing, three fish hatcheries and fish processing facilities. In 2008, 324 residents held commercial fishing permits.

Facilities and Services:
University of Alaska Southeast; full-service Bartlett Regional Hospital.
Newspapers: Daily Juneau Empire, Capital City Weekly.
Radio: KJNO AM-630; KINY AM-800; KBJZ FM-94.1; KFMG FM-100.7; KSRJ FM-102.7; KTOO FM-104.3 (Alaska Public Radio); KTKU FM-105.1; KSUP FM-106.3
TV: KTOO-TV 3 (PBS); KATH-TV 5 (NBC); KJUD-TV 8 (ABC); KXLJ-TV 13 (CBS).

Visitor Information:
Juneau Convention & Visitors Bureau, Centennial Building, 101 Egan Dr., 888-581-2201.
Web site: www.traveljuneau.com What to see and do in Juneau. Also look for information kiosks in Marine Park and the cruise ship terminal.

Juneau

"It's pretty common to see the governor walking to work."
—Juneau resident

Juneau, the first town founded in Alaska after the United States purchased the territory from Russia in 1867, was created by gold miners – and gold diggers seeking to strike it rich off the miners.

This was a fishing area used by Tlingits since time immemorial. In 1879, the famous naturalist John Muir visited Gastineau Channel. Muir's observations of mineralization on Mount Roberts drew great interest in Sitka, where German engineer George E. Pilz was developing a mine.

Pilz offered 100 Hudson's Bay blankets and work at the mine to any Tlingit tribe that could bring him promising ore samples. Chief Kowee of the Auk Tribe, which had villages near present-day Juneau, produced several such samples. Pilz grubstaked two prospectors, Joe Juneau and Richard T. Harris, and sent them off to Gastineau Channel. They returned empty-handed, but Pilz dispatched them again in October 1880, this time escorted by Chief Kowee. Kowee took the pair up Gold Creek to Silver Bow Basin and the mother lode. The boom was on.

Inside Passage Walking Tours

With the discovery of gold came a 160-acre town site – initially named Harrisburgh, but renamed Juneau in 1882.

Numerous mines sprang up on both sides of the channel, including the huge Alaska-Juneau mine built in 1916 on the side of Mount Roberts. The A-J became the largest operation of its kind, at its peak producing 13,000 tons of ore a day. Total production was more than 3.5 million ounces of gold, valued at over $80 million. By the 1930s, mining had declined, and the A-J closed in 1944.

Juneau's cost of living is about 15 percent higher than Seattle's.

Juneau's economy did not rely solely on gold mining, however. Fishing, canneries, transportation, trading services and a sawmill all contributed to its growth. Government operations became more important with statehood in 1959 and today 45 percent of Juneau's populace hold government jobs.

Situated below 3,576-foot Mount Juneau and 3,819-foot Mount Roberts, Juneau undoubtedly is one of the prettiest capital cities in the United States. The body of water in front of downtown is Gastineau Channel, where you sometimes can see whales,

along with sea kayakers, fishing boats and other maritime traffic. Across the channel is Douglas Island, part of the Alexander Archipelago, which protects the waterways of the Inside Passage from the Pacific Ocean.

With a population just topping 30,000, Alaska's third largest city is a place of contrasts. There's the hustle-bustle and deal-making of "The Session," when the Legislature comes to town. But there's also an informality that leaves room for a hand-printed "Closed for family fishing day" sign to be posted on a shop door on a sunny Sunday at the end of the tourist season. "It's pretty common to see the governor walking to work," noted a local. And when the big Fred Meyer grocery/department store opened, the whole town attended the festivities.

Because of fog and clouds, airplanes aren't always able to land in Juneau, so "overheading" is a common occurrence. Overheading can entail bouncing between Seattle and Anchorage for a day or more, without being able to land in Juneau. People have been known to overhead for three days, or get off the plane in Sitka and take the ferry to Juneau.

On clear nights look for the aurora borealis above Mt. Juneau.

Although it's on the mainland, you can't drive anywhere from Juneau. The city has 160 miles of roadways, but the three main routes all end in the forest. Driving "out the road" is popular on sunny days or when cabin fever strikes. The options are driving 5.5 miles south on Thane Road, 40 miles north on the Glacier Highway, or 13 miles on the North Douglas Highway, across the channel.

With the 17-million-acre Tongass National Forest at its back door, Juneau does not lack for outdoor-related recreational opportunities, from the active – hiking, biking, skiing, golf, kayaking, sailing, camping – to the more relaxed, such as the fireside lecture series at the Mendenhall Glacier Visitor Center in the wintertime. Juneau also is known for its arts and entertainment scene. Numerous art galleries feature the work of local artists. The city has a professional theater company – Perseverance Theatre – as well as community theater, opera and symphony.

Juneau has 1,900 registered boats, 1 for every 16 residents.

Community involvement and pride are evident in the downtown area, where flowers and a beautification program have spruced it up over the past 20 years. The city offers a charming blend of old and new, big and small.

FESTIVALS AND OTHER FUN

Juneau special events include: Wearable Art Extravaganza in February; the Alaska Folk Festival in early April, a week-long celebration featuring folk music and dance, concerts, workshops, and jam sessions; Juneau Jazz and Classics in May, a 10-day festival

featuring top jazz and classical musicians from around the world; Gold Rush Days in June, with mining and logging competitions, gold panning and a children's carnival; the Golden North Salmon Derby in August, with prizes for catching big fish, including $100,000 for one specially tagged salmon; Juneau Public Market gift show featuring statewide artists on Thanksgiving weekend; Gallery Walk, the first Friday of December, a holiday celebration with gallery receptions featuring artists and their work. Look in the *Juneau Empire* or *Capital City Weekly* or call the 24-hour events hotline 907-586-JUNO to find out what's going on while you're there.

DON'T MISS

Juneau attractions that you shouldn't miss:

- Mount Roberts Tramway (Stop #4), an 1,800-foot ascent from sea level, with spectacular views
- The Alaska State Museum (Stop # 21), with an excellent collection of Alaskana, Native cultures, Russian history and more
- Alaska's State Capitol (Stop #12), which offers free guided tours in the summer

- The view from the 8th floor terrace of the State Office Building (Stop #19)
- A visit to Juneau's drive-in glacier, Mendenhall, an awe-inspiring river of ice 3,000 years old, 12 miles long, 1 ½ miles wide and a hundred feet deep

Inside Passage Walking Tours

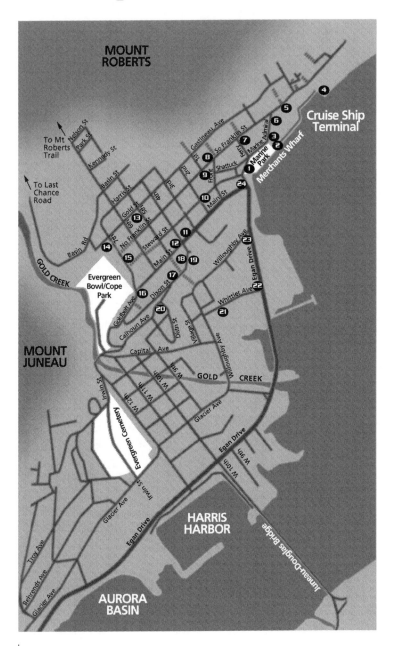

The Walking Tour

Inside Passage Walking Tours

Downtown Historic District with Mount Juneau in background.

Juneau Walking Tour

This walking tour through Alaska's capital city covers mostly flat terrain with a few hills, some of them steep. It takes you through Juneau's main downtown shopping area and to the State Capitol, Governor's Mansion, St. Nicholas Russian Orthodox Church, the city museum and the Alaska State Museum, with some great views and many historic buildings along the way. Estimated time is 2 to 2 ½ hours, or more, depending on stops along the way.

1 Begin at **Marine Park** on the central waterfront. Across Marine Way is the City and Borough of Juneau building (155 S. Seward Street), with Juneau artist Bill C. Ray's 61-foot mural of the Haida creation myth, **"Raven Discovers Mankind in a Clam Shell."**

Nearby is an information kiosk and local artist Ed Way's bronze sculpture **"Hard Rock Miner,"** depicting gold miners using a double jack drill. Watch the world go by from a large sheltered pavilion; free concerts on Fridays 7-8:30 p.m., June through mid-August.

From the sculpture, head toward the channel and turn left on the boardwalk.

2 Juneau's **Seawalk** affords great views: the Alaska-Juneau Mine ruins on the side of Mount Roberts; cruise ships, floatplanes, and fishing boats in Gastineau Channel. Barrels of flowers brighten the way spring through fall.

Inside Passage Walking Tours

Stop to Shop Juneau's downtown abounds in boutiques, galleries and gift shops, most notably along Franklin, Front and Seward Streets. Prices range from inexpensive to stratospheric. A few suggestions are:

Taku Smokeries, 550 S. Franklin St. Locally caught and smoked salmon; fresh frozen halibut and salmon; and "fish-ellaneous" gifts.

Decker Gallery, 233 S. Franklin St. A good place to find the works of Rie Munoz, a longtime Juneau artist who paints cheerful scenes of everyday Alaskan life.

Juneau Artists Gallery, 175 S. Franklin St. (Senate Building). A local co-operative selling watercolors, jewelry, etchings, photographs, art glass, ceramics, Ukrainian-style decorated eggs and pottery from more than 20 artists.

Wm. Spear Design, 174 S. Franklin St. (upstairs). A former lawyer/artist produces "some of the world's most wonderful enamels," a creative, colorful collection of enameled pins and zipper pulls.

Mt. Juneau Trading Post, 151 S. Franklin St. It's been here forever (well, almost). Northwest Coast art: totems, masks, argillite carvings. Ivory, jade, amber jewelry. Also Eskimo crafts, such as baskets, dolls, ivory carvings.

Annie Kaill's Fine Craft Gallery, 244 Front St. Hand-painted clothing, pottery, prints, and other creative, colorful gifts.

🚶 Proceed for 2 to 3 minutes along the Seawalk to the first large building on the left.

❸ The **Juneau Library** was built in 1988-89 atop a four-story parking garage, a design that made the cover of *Architectural Digest*. An elevator provides easy access to the fifth floor and its panoramic views. "**Transfiguration**," a stained glass window designed by Bruce Elliott, depicts salmon changing into figures from Tlingit mythology. 🏛 ♿

Outside on the channel side, there's a mural by Juneau artist Dan DeRoux of the steamship Ancon, based on an 1897 photograph, but with the faces of present-day Juneauites whose family histories date to the early 1900s. On the dock near the corner of the library is a bronze sculpture of Patsy Ann, an English bull terrier that greeted all arriving steamships in the 1930s and '40s. A plaque tells her story.

🚶 Continue along the Seawalk for 5 minutes, then turn left and cross the footbridge.

❹ The **Cruise Ship Terminal** houses an information center – a good place to find out what to see and do in Juneau. Public telephones. 🏛 ♿

To the right (south) is the lower terminal for the **Mount Roberts Tramway**. (See page 73 for information.)

The **Twisted Fish Company**, 550 S. Franklin St., is just beyond the tram terminal, across the parking lot. 𝖸 TWISTED FISH COMPANY

Inside Passage Walking Tours

Grabbing a Bite The following are a few suggested dining spots. The number indicates where to look for them along the walking tour.

Twisted Fish Company, 550 South Franklin Street (next to the tram terminal). (Stop #4) Watch floatplanes and savor the view along with freshly-caught fish and seafood. Largest wine bar in S.E. Alaska. Seasonal, May 1-Oct. 1. Open daily 11 a.m.-10 p.m. Lunch, dinner. Phone: 907-463-5033 $$-$$$

Tracy's King Crab Shack, 356 South Franklin Street (next to the library). (Between Stops #5 and #6) The "Best Legs in Town." Fresh King and Dungeness crab – legs, cakes, bisque and more – in a casual outdoor setting. Phone: 907-723-1811. Seasonal; open Mon.-Sun. 11 a.m.-7 p.m. $$-$$$

Sandpiper Café, 429 West Willoughby Ave. (Between Stops #20 and #21) One of the best breakfast spots in Juneau; creative, healthy and unusual dishes (Ostrich egg omelet for 10!). Generous portions. Open 6 a.m.-2 p.m. daily. Breakfast, lunch. Phone: 907-586-3150 $-$$

Zen, 51 Egan Drive. (Between Stops #23 and 24) Located in the Goldbelt Hotel. Combination of Asian fusion, Alaskan specialties and good ol' American breakfasts. Breakfast, lunch, dinner. Phone: 907-586-5075 $$-$$$

Hangar on the Wharf, 2 Marine Way. (Stop #24) A local favorite located in a former seaplane hangar with a great view of Gastineau Channel. Specializing in fresh local seafood. Lunch, dinner. Phone: 907-586-5018 $$-$$$

🏃 From the information center, go straight ahead to South Franklin Street and turn left.

5 Juneau's **main shopping area** – loaded with boutiques and galleries – is on South Franklin Street, along with a portion of the Downtown Historic District, with many late 19th- and early 20th-century buildings. On the first Friday of each month, many Juneau galleries and shops host exhibit openings, artist receptions and more.

The street's namesake is Howard Franklin, who led the miners' committee that laid out the original town site. The street runs along the original waterfront; the area on the water side has been filled in with rock "tailings" from the A-J Mine. Sidewalks here are grooved to resemble old-time boardwalks; some "sidewalks" are steep stairways up the mountainside.

The neighborhood across from the Cruise Ship Terminal was once known as "The Line," where "ladies of the evening" and speakeasies operated openly. Juneau's former red light district was Alaska's largest and longest-running, operating from 1881 to 1958.

🏃 Proceed up South Franklin Street for 3 to 4 minutes past the 0/parking garage to Admiral Way.

Tracy's King Crab Shack, 356 South Franklin Street, is located in an alley toward the pier, next to the library. **Y** TRACY'S KING CRAB SHACK

This side of the library features Ray Peck's **Eagle/Raven wrought-iron sculpture**, representing the main clans of the Tlingit culture.

Inside Passage Walking Tours

⑥ Across Admiral Way from the library is the rollicking **Red Dog Saloon**, 278 South Franklin Street, complete with swinging doors, sawdust floors, honky-tonk music and assorted oddities such as Wyatt Earp's pistol, which he left in Juneau when traveling to Nome.

🚶 Cross Admiral Way and proceed along the left-hand side of Franklin Street about 10 minutes (or more if you stop to shop) to Front Street.

⑦ Among the **historic buildings** along Franklin Street between Admiral Way and Front Street are:

- The Senate Building (175 S. Franklin Street), built in 1898 and now a shopping mall.
- The turreted Alaska Steam Laundry Building (174 S. Franklin Street), constructed in 1901 and on the National Register of Historic Places. It's also a shopping mall. Wander its hallways to see a collection of photographs dating back to the 1880s.
- The Alaskan Hotel (167 S. Franklin Street), built in 1913 and also on the National Register. It is Juneau's oldest continuously operating hotel. Note the ornate tin ceiling if you drop in; its bar is a favorite local watering hole and a good place to try an Alaskan Amber or Pale Ale from Juneau's own microbrewery.

A U.S. Postal Station is located at 145 S. Franklin Street, #A.

✉

🚶 Continue to the clock at Franklin and Front Streets.

OPTION:

🚶🏃 *From the clock, walk a block and a half up Franklin to the Westmark Baranof Hotel.*

On the way, you'll pass the Elks Hall, built in 1908. The first Territorial Legislature met here in 1913.

The Westmark Baranof Hotel, 105 Franklin Street, is named for Lord Aleksandr Baranov, governor of Russian America (who probably never visited the Juneau area). Built in 1938-39, the 10-story Art Moderne-style hotel cost $550,000 to build – hard to come by during the Depression – and was Alaska's most modern hotel. Damaged by fire in 1984, the hotel has been restored to its original décor and is on the National Register. Its public rooms feature original paintings by famous Alaskan masters, including Sydney M. Laurence, Eustace Paul Ziegler and Don Clever. Hobnob in the Bubble Room with Alaska pol-

The Bird Man of Juneau

One night in 1909, a man was shot and killed in Juneau. Not an uncommon event in a rough-and-tumble mining town. However, this shooting was committed by one Robert Stroud, whose later crimes earned him a life sentence at Alcatraz Federal Penitentiary in San Francisco Bay, where he became known as "The Bird Man of Alcatraz" because of his dedication to learning about and caring for birds.

Stroud killed the Alaskan Hotel's bartender at a little house that used to stand behind what is now an office building at the corner of Fourth and Franklin Streets.

iticians during the legislative session, which begins in January.

An ATM is located at Alaska Pacific Bank, 301 North Franklin Street. 🏧

🚶 *Retrace your steps back downhill to Front Street, turn right at the clock.*

❽ Across Franklin Street from the clock is **Gunakadeit Park** (pronounced Goo-na'-ka-date), which takes its name from a mythical Tlingit sea animal that represents good fortune and prosperity to those who see it.

🚶 *From the clock, continue along Front Street one block to Seward Street.*

❾ **Front Street** traces Juneau's former high-tide line; buildings on the left-hand side originally were built on pilings over the beach.

Among Front Street's historic buildings are:

• The Imperial Saloon, 241 Front Street, built in 1891 and the oldest saloon in Alaska, operating continuously at the same location. The pressed tin ceiling and the back bar date from 1908. A brothel was once located upstairs; occasionally, the madam would direct an unwelcome customer to a certain door in the side of the building – on pilings at the time – and he'd step out right into the channel.

• 225 Front Street, built c. 1895, operated for decades as a hardware store.

• Lawyer Jack Hellenthal built his namesake building at 220 Front Street in 1916.

• The 1939 20th Century Gross Building, 210 Front St., with geometric Art Deco designs above its windows.

- The Queen Anne-style Valentine Building, 202 Front Street, was constructed in 1904 and 1913 by Emery Valentine, a jeweler and prominent civic leader. On the National Register, it was restored in 1982. If you drop in at the drugstore, check out the ornate gilded ceiling.
- The 1896 Lewis Building, 130 Front St. Now a McDonald's restaurant, it housed a bank until 1925.

An ATM is located at the First National Bank, 238 Front Street. 🟥

↟↟ Turn right on Seward Street and proceed up the hill one block.

🔟 The five-story **Goldstein Building**, 130 Seward St., originated in 1914 as fur buyer Charles Goldstein's department store. The building also housed the Territorial Legislature and Executive Office from 1925 to 1931

Around the corner to the left is the **Messerschmidt Building**, 120 Second Street. There has been a bakery on this site since 1890. The current building, constructed in 1914, was a bakery for years and is now the Silverbow Inn and Restaurant, which also runs a bakery.

↟↟ Cross Second Street and continue up one block to Third Street.

ATMs are located at Wells Fargo, 123 Seward St., and Key Bank, 234 Seward Street. 🟥

The Key Bank (former Behrends Bank) building on the corner

of Third and Seward was built by B.M. Behrends, who arrived in Juneau in 1887 and operated a variety store. When the Bank of Juneau failed in 1896, Behrends offered banking services to his customers and built this bank in 1914.

🚶 *Turn right on Third Street one block to Main Street. Turn right up the hill.*

⓫ At mid-block there's a life-sized bronze sculpture of a brown bear, **"Windfall Fisherman,"** created by Juneau artist R.T. "Skip" Wallen to commemorate the 25th anniversary of Alaska statehood. It's in the courtyard of the **Dimond Courthouse**, named for John H. Dimond (1918-1985), justice of the original Supreme Court of Alaska.

From the sculpture, there's an excellent view of the marble-columned Alaska State Capitol. 📷

🚶 *Continue up the hill and cross Fourth Street to the Capitol Building.*

⓬ **Alaska's State Capitol** was completed in 1931 as the Federal and Territorial Building, using marble mined at Tokeen on Prince of Wales Island near Ketchikan. Marble lines the lobby; there's

also a marble bear sculpture. The Liberty Bell replica in front of the building was donated to the state in 1950 during a U.S. Savings Bond drive.

Free, 30-minute guided tours are available from mid-May to mid-Sept.; Mon.-Fri. 8:30 a.m.-5 p.m.; Sat.-Sun. 9:30 a.m.-4 p.m. The Governor's Office is on the third floor. The Alaska State Legislature meets on the second floor beginning in January. Floor sessions start about 11 a.m. week-

days. Visitor galleries for House and Senate are on the second floor. 🚻

∧☆ *After exiting the Capitol Building, proceed left half a block to Seward Street, turn left for a fairly steep block to Fifth Street, and then turn right for a block and a half.*

⓭ On the National Register of Historic Places and one of Juneau's most-photographed buildings, **St. Nicholas Russian Orthodox Church**, 326 5th St., is the oldest original Russian Orthodox church in Southeast Alaska, built in 1894. The small (27-foot diameter) octagonal building symbolizes the seven days of the week and an "eighth day" of rest. Its entry is on the opposite side from the street to conform to a church dictate that the altar be placed toward the east. Photographs are permitted inside the church, which has many beautiful works of art, including 18th-century icons. The church is open for informal tours weekdays during the summer; a donation is requested. Visitors are welcome to attend Sunday services at 9 a.m. year-round. Call 907-586-1023 for additional information. 📷

Across Gold Street on Fifth is the Roman Catholic Cathedral of the Nativity of the Blessed Virgin Mary, built in 1910. One block away, at 411 Gold Street is Holy Trinity Episcopal Church, constructed in 1896.

∧☆ *After exiting the Orthodox church, return to Fifth Street. Continue to the corner and turn left up Gold Street for two very steep blocks to Seventh Street and turn left.*

OPTION:

𝆐𝆑 *For a detour to Starr Hill, turn to the right on Sixth Street. From Gold Street, walk three short but steep blocks to Kennedy Street.*

Starr Hill is one of Juneau's oldest neighborhoods, named for early-day builder Frank Starr. Kennedy Street is the namesake of Irish immigrant Dan Kennedy, who arrived in Juneau in 1880 and served for many years as Juneau's night watchman and constable.

At the corner of Sixth and Kennedy is **Chicken Yard Park**, with a small sculpture of a nun feeding chickens. Now a playground, it once was the chicken yard for a convent.

Many of Starr Hill's homes were built to be rented to mining families. Prime examples are the Kennedy Street Mineworkers Houses, listed on the National Register of Historic Places. On Kennedy Street, between Sixth and Fifth, the six formerly identical Craftsman-style bungalows built in 1913 have taken on individual looks through the years.

A bit farther along Kennedy, at Fifth Street, is a charming wooden sculpture of children linking arms in a circle. Titled **"Living Together in Peace,"** it sits near the top of a stairway between Kennedy and East streets.

𝆐𝆑 *Return to Gold Street either by taking the stairway down to East Street and then walking*

right to Sixth or by walking back on Kennedy and then down Sixth Street to Gold Street. At Gold Street, turn right uphill to Seventh and turn left.

Two historic homes are on Sixth Street, between Gold and Seward streets:

• The J.M. Davis House, 202 6th St., constructed in 1893 by Frances Brooks Davis, a wealthy English painter who came to Juneau in 1891, and J. Montgomery Davis, an English bookkeeper and assistant manager of the Nowell Gold Mining Co., whom she married in 1892.

• The Frances House, 137 6th St., built in 1898 and owned by U.S. Attorney General of Alaska John Rustgard from 1910 to 1927, when Frances Davis bought it and moved it to its present location.

---

14 The **Chicken Ridge Historic District**, which includes the area along Seventh, Goldbelt, and Dixon Streets (plus the upper portion of Main Street between Sixth and Seventh) is another of Juneau's oldest neighborhoods, first settled in 1893. It was named by early-day miners, who hunted grouse and ptarmigan ("chickens" to them) in the area. The ridge separates the **Evergreen Bowl/Cope Park** recreation area and downtown Juneau. Numerous large, late 19th- and early 20th-century homes dot the neighborhood.

Continue one and a half blocks to 213 Seventh Street.

15 The **Wickersham House**, 213 Seventh Street, was built in 1898 for Frank Hammond, superintendent of the Sheep Creek Mining Co. In 1928, the home was purchased by Judge James

Inside Passage Walking Tours

Wickersham, a noted Alaskan lawyer, politician, historian, author and statehood proponent, who lived here until his death in 1939. As Alaska's third delegate to Congress, Wickersham worked to obtain a territorial legislature (1912), a railroad linking Anchorage and Fairbanks (1914), and Mount McKinley National Park and the agricultural college which became the University of Alaska (1917). On the National Register, the home is owned by the State of Alaska. Today the stories of Judge Wickersham and Alaska's early days are told through historical photographs, Alaskan artifacts, memorabilia and period furnishings. The nonprofit Wickersham Society operates tours in the summer. Summer hours: Daily except Wed., 1-5 p.m. Winter: Open by appointment only. Admission: $1. Call 907-586-9001 for information.

Next door, at 227 Seventh Street, is the **Faulkner House**, a Colonial Revival-style home built in 1914 for Herbert Faulkner, a deputy U.S. marshal and lawyer.

Fish as Airborne Hazards

Juneau has the distinction of being the location of the only recorded mid-air collision between a jet and a steelhead. On the morning of March 31, 1987, an Alaska Airlines Boeing 737 was taking off from Juneau International Airport. The ascending jet crossed paths with a bald eagle that had just caught its breakfast: a steelhead trout. The startled eagle dropped its fish, which smacked into the airplane with a "thud" as the eagle flew off unharmed. The jet was inspected at its next stop and found to be undamaged by its close encounter with the fish. As the airline's employee publication put it: "The sole crime was slime." The fish story attracted national attention, though, especially since the next day was April Fools' Day.

Across the street, at 206 Seventh Street, is the **Thane-Holbrook House**, a bungalow built c.1916 for Bartlett Thane, manager and director of the Alaska Gastineau Mining Co.

Around the corner from the Wickersham House is a public stairway – the Seward Street stairs – down to Sixth and Fifth Streets. (Please respect adjoining private property.) Trees obscure the view from the top of the stairs.

From the Wickersham House continue along Seventh to Main Street and turn left down the hill.

OPTION: Before heading down Main Street, take a short detour for a scenic view.

Cross Main and continue on Seventh, which curves and becomes Goldbelt Avenue. Go another half a block to the West Eighth Street Stairs.

From the stairs, you'll have a view of Douglas Island, Gastineau Channel, the Juneau-Douglas Bridge, and West Juneau. 📷

Retrace your steps back to Seventh and Main.

🔟 The **intersection of Seventh and Main** is a great spot from which to take photos. From here, you can easily see why Juneau is often referred to as **"Little San Francisco."** 📷

On Main Street hill, you'll pass through a picturesque neighborhood with some of the oldest homes in Juneau. Most porches and yards are bright with flowers in the summer.

Continue downhill to Fifth Street and turn right half a block to a footbridge.

17 From the center of the **foot-bridge over Calhoun Avenue**, there's an excellent view of the Governor's Mansion, the Calhoun Avenue Promenade (built in 1995), Gastineau Channel, the Juneau-Douglas Bridge, and Douglas Island. 📷

Calhoun Avenue follows a trail that once linked downtown Juneau with the Auke Indian community, over the side of the hill. The street was named for Juneau pioneers John and Mary Calhoun, whose dairy was on the site of the Governor's Mansion.

Retrace your steps back to Main Street and turn right down the hill to Fourth Street.

18 The **Juneau-Douglas City Museum,** on the corner of Fourth and Main Streets, has an extensive collection of mining relics and other artifacts. A 5-by-7-foot relief map orients visitors to Juneau's topography. Videos tell about the founding of Juneau and Douglas and helpful staff and volunteers answer questions. The Museum Shop sells books, souvenirs, and collectibles.

Open daily May-Sept. 9 a.m.-5 p.m., weekdays; 10 a.m.-5 p.m. weekends. Oct.-April, open Thurs.-Sat., 10 a.m.-4 p.m.; other times by appointment. Summer admission is $4; winter admission free. Call 907-586-3572 for more information. 🚻 ♿

After leaving the museum, cross Fourth Street and continue to the right to the large building.

⑲ The 11-story **State Office Building** was constructed in 1974, nestled into the side of Courthouse Hill, named for the federal courthouse that stood here from 1903 until the early 1970s. Known locally as "The SOB," it houses the Alaska State Library, including the state's historical library (hours are 10 a.m.-4:30 p.m. weekdays), as well as state offices. From Fourth Street, enter the 8th-floor atrium housing the **"Old Witch Totem Pole,"** carved in the late 1800s, and a 1928 **Kimball pipe organ**, a reminder of the silent films that entertained early-day Juneauites. Drop in for the free organ concert at noon each Friday.

The large terrace on the opposite side of the building affords excellent views. 📷

The elevators at the back of the atrium are the quickest way to get from "upper Juneau" at the Fourth Street level to "lower Juneau" at the Willoughby Avenue level. Keep in mind that the building is locked on weekends. 🚻 ♿

🥾 *Exit the State Office Building from the Fourth Street doors (where you came in) and turn left on Fourth, which curves and becomes Calhoun Avenue. Continue for two blocks along the Calhoun Avenue Promenade, which has benches and good views.* 📷

⑳ At Calhoun Avenue and Distin Street is the Colonial Revival-style **Governor's Mansion**, listed on the National Register of Historic Places. The official residence of Alaska's governor, the home was built in 1912, the year Alaska became a territory of the United States and Juneau was named its capital. The Governor's Totem Pole was carved in 1939-40 by Charlie Tagook and William Brown of Klukwan and Saxman; its figures tell the Tlingit story of the creation of the stars, sunlight and tides, and the population of earth by land animals, sea mammals and mosquitoes. The original building cost $40,000 – including furniture. In 1983, the mansion was renovated to its original décor – at a cost of $2 million. The 14,400-square-foot building has 35 rooms, including 10 bathrooms, six bedrooms and eight fireplaces. The personal living quarters are on the second floor. No regular tours are offered, however there's a public open house in early December and private tours may be arranged through the Office of the Governor (call 907-465-3500 for information).

Retrace your steps back on Calhoun to the pedestrian overpass. Take the 90 stairs down to Willoughby Avenue. Or, go back to the State Office Building and all the way through the atrium, then take the elevator down to Willoughby (weekday option only). Once you're on Willoughby, turn to the right for 2 to 5 minutes, depending on which option you choose, around a curve to Whittier Street and turn left one block to the Alaska State Museum (See Stop #21).

About a block past Whittier, at 429 W. Willoughby Ave., is the **Sandpiper Café**. ✗ SANDPIPER CAFÉ

OPTION: For an alternate route to the **Alaska State Museum** that takes you through **Evergreen Cemetery** and past the Federal Building and **two historic monuments**:

Continue past the Governor's Mansion on Calhoun Avenue, downhill for about 5 minutes. Calhoun becomes Irwin Street on the other side of Gold Creek. Follow Irwin as it veers to the right, into the entrance of the cemetery.

Evergreen Cemetery is the resting place of many Juneau pioneers, including the city's co-founders, Joseph Juneau and Richard T. Harris, who lie buried across the path from each other less than a minute into the cemetery. On other graves, you may recognize names from Juneau's streets and historic buildings.

Continue through the cemetery for another 5 minutes to Glacier Avenue and turn left.

Facing Glacier Avenue is a **monument to Clan Leader Kowee** of the Auke Tribe, who led Juneau and Harris to the October 1880 gold discovery that, in turn, led to the settlement of the city of Juneau. The monument marks the approximate location where Kowee's body was cremated according to Tlingit custom of the time.

Continue on Glacier Avenue for about seven blocks to Whittier Street.

You'll pass the nine-story **Federal Building**. A large fountain featuring Thomas Austin Harly's **"Diving Pelicans"** sculpture stands in the plaza. Pelicans are not indigenous to Alaska; the proper artwork was an eagle that was mistakenly sent to Florida.

The U.S. Post Office is located in the lobby of the Federal Building. ✉ 🕐 ♿

Inside Passage Walking Tours

Just before you cross Gold Creek you'll see the **Founders Memorial** commemorating the founding of Juneau.

⚴ _Take a right on Whittier Street for one block to the Alaska State Museum._

㉑ The **Alaska State Museum**, 395 Whittier Street, built in 1967 on fill from mine "tailings," has an excellent collection of Alaskana, featuring the state's Native cultures, Russian history, mining and fishing, a wildlife display and traveling exhibits.

Begun as a territorial museum in 1900, the museum now has

more than 31,000 artifacts and works of art. Its two floors are connected by a ramp that curves around an atrium and an "eagle tree" exhibit including a nest and seven bald eagles at various life stages. Other natural history exhibits along the ramp include totem poles, a petroglyph, plant

life and brown bears. On the main floor, suspended from the ceiling is a six-foot-diameter, interactive globe developed by the National Oceanic and Atmospheric Administration that illustrates the earth's weather and geologic systems. The Museum Shop sells Alaska Native art, publications, graphics and educational products.

On the lawn is **"Nimbus,"** a modern sculpture that generated much controversy when originally installed in front of the Dimond Courthouse. The Legislature ordered it moved.

Open daily mid-May to mid-Sept.; 8:30 a.m.-5:30 p.m. Mid-Sept. to mid-May open Tues.-Sat.; 10 a.m.-4 p.m. Closed Memorial Day, 4th of July and Labor Day. Admission: Summer $5; winter

$3; children 18 and under, free. Docents are available to interpret exhibits for summer visitors. Call 907-465-2901 for more information. ⬚ ♿

🚶 From the museum, continue to the right on Whittier Street to Egan Drive.

㉒ On the corner is the **Juneau Arts & Culture Center**, 350 Whittier St., which has a gallery featuring local artists. From mid-June to mid-Aug. events include the Juneau Artists Market, Sat. 10 a.m.-4 p.m.; Sun.-Mon. 11 a.m.-4 p.m.; and the Juneau Farmers Market, Sat. 10 a.m.-noon.

🚶 Turn left on Egan Drive for a block to the convention center.

㉓ The **Juneau Convention & Visitors Bureau** is located in **Centennial Hall**, 101 Egan Dr. (named for Alaska's first state governor, William A. Egan). You'll find information on what to see and do in Juneau. Call 888-581-2201 for information. (Also look

---

Town Where the Takus Blow

During the fall and winter, Juneauites experience one of Alaska's more infamous weather phenomena: the taku winds. Bone-chilling takus scream down off the Juneau Icefield at up to 100 miles per hour, packing enough power to have once punched a 2-by-4 board through the wall of a house. Because of the accompanying power outages, every local resident has at least one Thanksgiving or Christmas Day storm story, complete with details on how they cooked the turkey during the power outage.

for information kiosks in Marine Park and the cruise ship terminal.) Web site: www.traveljuneau.com. 🕮 ♿

Across the street from Centennial Hall is **"the subport,"** named for the submarines that docked there during World War II. Now it's home to the U.S. Coast Guard and National Marine Fisheries Service.

🚶🏃 *From Centennial Hall, it's 3 blocks to the end of the walking tour. Turn left on Egan Drive, which becomes Marine Way at Main Street.*

Located in the Goldbelt Hotel, 51 Egan Drive, is the restaurant **Zen**. 🍴 ZEN

OPTION:

🚶🏃 *Turn left at Main Street and walk three blocks to West Third Street, turn left and go up Telephone Hill.*

Telephone Hill was named after William Webster, who placed Juneau's first telephone line across Gastineau Channel in 1883, connecting his home (Juneau's oldest, built in 1882) on top of the hill to his store in Douglas. The Webster family ran the telephone company until the 1950s.

🚶🏃 *West Third curves and becomes Dixon Street. Continue about 2 blocks to a dead end.*

The end of Dixon has good views of the channel, boat and floatplane traffic, and cruise ships. 📷

🥾 *Retrace your steps back down the hill. Or, continue to the left, down a set of stairs. Turn right on Main Street for a block back to Marine Way and turn left.*

---

24 At Main Street and Marine Way is the headquarters of the **Sealaska Corporation**, one of 12 regional corporations formed under the Alaska Native Claims Settlement Act of 1971.

Hangar on the Wharf is located on the waterfront. ✗ HANGAR ON THE WHARF

🥾 *Walk 2 blocks back to Marine Park and the end of the walking tour.*

Mural of the Haida creation myth, "Raven Discovers Mankind in a Clam Shell."

Clockwise from top left: office building displays Alaska flag motif; monument to Clan Leader Kowee; Juneau's Red Dog Saloon; "Living Together in Peace" sculpture on Starr Hill.

Getting Out of Town

HIGH ON THE VIEW: MOUNT ROBERTS TRAMWAY

Soar with the eagles 1,800 feet above Juneau aboard the Mount Roberts Tramway. Two enclosed 60-person gondolas depart every 12 to 15 minutes from the terminal, 490 S. Franklin St., next to the cruise ship dock.

The tramway runs to the upper terminal, Mountain House (Shaa Hit) recreation and cultural complex, featuring a weather-protected observation deck with panoramic views. Other attractions include the Timberline Bar & Grill; Raven Eagle Gifts; the Chilkat Theater showing the 30-minute film Seeing Daylight, about Southeast Alaska Native cultures; a nature center; Juneau Raptor Center bald eagle display; and the Mount Roberts trail system. Open May-September; Mon.-Fri. 8 a.m.-9 p.m.; Sat.-Sun. 9 a.m.-9 p.m. Tickets include all-day unlimited rides, the film and the eagle display. Rates are $27 for adults; $13.50 for children 6-12; children 5 and under, free.

TAKE A HIKE: MOUNT ROBERTS TRAIL

One of Juneau's most accessible trails is the one up Mount Roberts, which begins on Starr Hill at the east end of Sixth Street. The trail ascends 4.5 miles to the 3,819-foot summit, for spectacular views. It is moderately difficult, but well maintained, with plenty of places to stop off and enjoy the view. For a quickie wilderness experience and a great photo opportunity, there's an excellent viewpoint about 20 minutes up. At the 1,760-foot level, you come to the restaurant at the top of the Mount Roberts Tramway. (See page vii for hiking cautions.)

TAKE A HIKE: BASIN ROAD
AND LAST CHANCE MINING MUSEUM

Basin Road offers a level, mile-long hike into the hills behind Juneau to Last Chance Basin. Walk up Gold Street to the top, turn right, then left at the next corner onto Basin Road. At the end of the dirt road, go right over a footbridge. The Last Chance Mining Museum is in the compressor house of the Alaska-Juneau Gold Mining Co., which operated from 1912 until 1944. Listed on the National Register of Historic Places and Alaska Gold Rush Proper-

Juneau Bear-y Tales

Alaska's capital city is literally at the edge of the wilderness. There's wildlife galore, but the black bears that regularly wander into town get the most attention. (Seems Juneau was built on an historic bear migration route and the bears haven't forgotten they were here first.) From March to October, police typically receive dozens of bear sighting reports. Bears might be spotted simply walking down the street minding their own business. Or there might be a closer encounter – possibly plundering someone's kitchen after entering through an open window. In 1993, a bear appeared at the front door of a downtown supermarket. And, in 1991, a cub wandered into the hospital's emergency room.

Local TV announcements warn about "garbage bears." One downtown neighborhood has "bear monitors" who ensure the animals "safe passage" or call the police if necessary. Public trash bins downtown have special latches to keep bears out. Residents commonly put their garbage in the freezer until pickup day so it doesn't attract bears. And, "out the road" in the Mendenhall Valley, an ultra-heavy-duty fence surrounds an elementary school – not to keep the kids in, but to keep the bears out.

ties, it has the world's largest Ingersoll-Rand air compressor with its 11-ton wheel, mining equipment, minerals display and the Alaska-Juneau Adit, an underground exhibit of hard rock mining. (Other mine buildings may be in disrepair and should not be entered.) Admission is $4; special rates for private tours and groups. Open daily mid-May to late September, 9:30 a.m.-12:30 p.m. and 3-6:30 p.m. or by appointment. Call 907-586-5338 for information.

JUNEAU'S BACKYARD GLACIER: MENDENHALL

Just 13 miles from downtown, Juneau's backyard glacier, Mendenhall, is an awe-inspiring sight. A frozen river 12 miles long, 1 ½ miles wide, and a hundred feet deep, Mendenhall emanates from the 1,500-square-mile Juneau Icefield, located just over the mountains behind the city. The visitors' center features an excellent view of the glacier's face, telescopes for a close-up look, a three-dimensional topographical map of the entire icefield, guided nature

View from Starr Hill overlooking Chicken Yard Park (foreground) toward Douglas Island (background).

hikes, and video programs. Call 907-789-0097 for information.

You can drive from Juneau to the glacier via the Glacier Highway and Mendenhall Loop Road. Or, take a Capital Transit bus to the Mendenhall Glacier Spur Road and from there, walk the 1.4 miles to the visitors center. Information available at the Juneau Convention & Visitors Bureau, Centennial Building, 101 Egan Dr., or from the bus company, 907-789-6901. You can also hire a taxi for a flat rate (EverGreen Taxi, 907-586-2121, or Juneau Taxi & Tours, 907-790-4511)

Several flightseeing and helicopter operators offer the chance to view, or even walk on, the icefield. Also, a visit to Mendenhall Glacier is included on most city tours (available on board cruise ships). Call Gray Line of Alaska, 907-586-3773 or 800-544-2206, for city tour information; Wings of Alaska, 907-789-0790, for flightseeing; Temsco Helicopters, 907-789-9501, or ERA Helicopters, 907-586-2030, for heli-touring.

ICEBERG EXTRAVAGANZA:
GLACIER BAY NATIONAL PARK

Two hundred years ago, when Captain George Vancouver was exploring the area, Glacier Bay was just a dent in a 4,000-foot-thick wall of ice along the shore of Icy Strait, 50 miles from Juneau. Today, visitors can travel 60 miles up the bay from the park headquarters at Bartlett Cove, viewing 12 tidewater glaciers along the way. This 3.3-million-acre park also features humpback whales, harbor seals, and a multitude of birds, including puffins.

For information, contact Glacier Bay National Park and Preserve, 907-697-2230; Glacier Bay Tours and Cruises, 800-451-5952; or check with the Juneau Convention & Visitors Bureau, Centennial Building, 101 Egan Dr., 888-581-2201. Many cruise ships also visit Glacier Bay or offer shore excursions to the park.

At right: historic exhibit in 1898 Mascot Saloon building.

Skagway

Skagway at a Glance

Population:
Municipality of Skagway: 846 (5.1% Alaska Natives); 1,300+ in summer, with seasonal workers; 52.2% Men; 47.8% Women; Visitors: 1 million annually

Geography:
Municipality of Skagway: 452.4 sq. mi. of land; 11.9 sq. mi. of water
Location: At the head of Taiya Inlet at the northernmost end of Lynn Canal on the mainland of Southeast Alaska, 15 highway miles south of the U.S./Canada border; 90 air miles northeast of Juneau and nearly 1,000 air miles north of Seattle.

Weather:
Average summer temperatures: 45-67° F
Average winter temperatures: 18-37° F
Annual precipitation: 26"

Primary Industries:
Tourism ($40 million industry; 339 cruise ship visits), retail shops and services, government, railroad (operated seasonally), trans-shipment of freight, fuel and lead/zinc ore

Facilities and Services:
Skagway School (about 100 students, grades K-12); Dahl Memorial Clinic (nearest full-service hospital is in Juneau).
Newspaper: biweekly Skagway News.
TV: Cable service.
Radio: KHNS-FM 91.9.

Visitor Information:
Skagway Visitor Information Center, in the Arctic Brotherhood Hall, on Broadway St. between Second and Third Avenues; 907- 983-2854.

Klondike Gold Rush National Historical Park Visitors Center, Second and Broadway, 907-983-2921.
Information, programs and displays on the gold rush, hiking the Chilkoot Trail. Open May-Sept. only.

Skagway

*"We are a living historical community. We didn't recreate
Broadway in some kind of urban renewal project."*
—*Skagway resident*

The Klondike Gold Rush gave birth to Skagway in a two-year
frenzy, during which a handful of homesteaders exploded into as
many as 15,000 gold-crazed stampeders. And the gold rush keeps
Skagway alive today. These days, however, the stampeders come
from cruise ships and ferries.

Skagway is the genuine article. "We are a living historical
community. We didn't recreate Broadway in some kind of urban
renewal project," says a local. Narrow, false-fronted buildings line
Broadway's boardwalks. Many structures in the 6-by-2-block historic district are original; a few are even said to harbor ghosts. As
you stroll the boardwalks, you can imagine lively tunes from a
honky-tonk piano, the clamor of a thousand excited voices, maybe a gunshot or two – echoes of the past in this historic "Gateway
to the Klondike."

Summer is Skagway's season. And when it's over, the town
shuts down. Only a few businesses stay open during the winter

months, and nearly a third of the population leaves town for warmer climes. "After 14- and 16-hour days in the summer, they just want to kick back," explains a resident.

Once, only the hunting camps of the Chilkoot Tlingits were here. The Chilkoots zealously guarded access to the steep, rugged route over Chilkoot Pass, the ancient "grease trail" used for trading oily hooligan fish for furs and copper from the Tagish Athabaskans in the interior. When the trail was opened to others in 1880, the Chilkoots quickly adapted, securing the lucrative business of packing prospectors' outfits over the pass.

Early in 1887, Captain William "Billy" Moore bushwhacked his way along a "secret" route up the Skagway River valley and White Pass was opened. Moore was convinced it would be the primary route to the Yukon, where he predicted a major gold strike would occur. In anticipation, he built a cabin, sawmill and wharf on Skagway Bay.

Although Alaska had been "dry" since its purchase from Russia, Gold Rush-era Skagway boasted 70 saloons and 3 breweries.

Nothing much happened until 1896, when three prospectors – "Skookum" Jim Mason, George Washington Carmack and Tagish Charlie – made an incredibly rich gold strike on a tributary of the Klondike River. It was the middle of nowhere – but not for long. Local prospectors poured in, staking the creeks feeding the Klondike. But it was nearly a year before news of the strike reached the outside world.

On July 15, 1897, a ship steamed into San Francisco bearing a couple of dozen prospectors and their gold. Two days later, another ship arrived in Seattle, this time with 68 miners. And the world took notice. "A ton of gold!" trumpeted a local newspaper.

All of North America, then in the depths of a severe economic depression, was electrified. By nightfall, the great Klondike Gold Rush had begun.

Gold-crazed men and women booked passage for the Klondike, even though most had no idea where it was. Seattle, a frontier outpost of about 67,000, lost 10,000 residents that first summer, but prosperity soon doubled its population as merchants sold all manner of goods to the "argonauts."

The first boatload of stampeders hit Skagway on July 29. Overnight, a tent city sprang up. With only one U.S. deputy marshal in the entire region, Skagway was a lawless town. A commander of Canada's North West Mounted Police dubbed it "the roughest place in the world, little better than a hell on earth." It boasted some 70 saloons, brothels did a brisk business, shootings were commonplace. Jefferson Randolph "Soapy" Smith and his gang held sway for several months, until Smith died in a famous shootout with town surveyor Frank Reid.

Although Skagway's population officially is 52.2% male and 47.8% female, "in the winter it seems more like 15 or 16 men to each woman."

By the spring of 1898, tramways crossed Chilkoot Pass, and Brackett's Wagon Road approached the summit of White Pass. Around the same time, a deal was struck to build the White Pass & Yukon Route. With the railroad's completion, Chilkoot Pass was no longer needed.

Then, as quickly as it had begun, the gold rush was over. With its end in 1900, Skagway might have become a ghost town if not for the WP&YR, which provided a vital connection to Whitehorse and mines in the Yukon. The railroad was Skagway's economic mainstay until 1982, when it shut down. The little town of Skagway was brought to its knees. "They laid off 185 people and within two years 400 people lost their jobs," recalls a former employee.

Tourism saved Skagway. In 1976, Congress had created Klondike Gold Rush National Historical Park and restoration of Skagway's gold rush-era buildings, many of which were boarded up and in danger of falling down, began in earnest. Then, in 1988, the WP&YR reopened as an excursion train.

Today, the historic buildings – many housing bustling shops and restaurants – have been colorfully restored. Bountiful gardens boost Skagway's fame as the "Garden City of Alaska." A million visitors pass through each summer. Tourism has expanded to offer backcountry hiking, mountain biking and other "soft adventure" tours. The shipment of ore, fuel, and freight via the Klondike Highway to and from Canada bolsters the economy.

Skagway is like a big shopping mall – it's an easy town and a flat town.

Its isolation and the seasonal nature of its economy lend a zany zest to life in Skagway. Says one local: "People get a little crazy and do things like a chainsaw-throwing contest or bowling on Broadway. The imagination in this town is a wonderful thing."

FESTIVALS AND OTHER FUN

Skagway happenings of note include: The Buckwheat Ski Classic, 4th weekend in March, a classic-style cross country ski race designed for the "lazy, the infirm and a few who are fast"; International Mini Folk Festival, 4th weekend in April, featuring musicians from the Yukon and Southeast Alaska; party down with the locals at the Summer Solstice Party and Midnight Picnic; Soapy

Smith's Wake every July 8; the Eastern Star Flower Show and Gold Rush Garden Club Competition in August; the Klondike Trail of '98 Road Relay Race covering 115 miles from Skagway to White-horse in September; and the "Victorian Yuletide" celebration and ball in early December. For more, look in the *Skagway News* or call the Skagway Convention and Visitors Bureau at 907-983-2855.

DON'T MISS

Skagway attractions not to miss:

- The Klondike Gold Rush Historical Park visitors center (Stop #1 on the walking tour), for giant photographs and excellent displays about the gold rush.
- A ride on the White Pass & Yukon Route (Stop #1). Travel in comfort aboard vintage railroad cars and imagine what the stampeders endured making their way over the pass.
- The Red Onion (Stop #3), for ragtime music and a local crowd.
- Skagway Museum & Archives (also known as the Trail of '98 Museum) (Stop #14). Showcases a fine collection of Alaska Native artwork and a fascinating Gold Rush collection of memorabilia, artifacts and tools.
- Corrington Museum of Alaskan History, (Between Stops #10 and 11) inside a gift shop at 525 Broadway, has interesting displays of trade beads, baleen baskets, scrimshaw and Gold Rush photos.
- "The Days of '98 Show with Soapy Smith" performed since 1927 at the Eagles Hall, 590 Broadway (Stop #11). A lively melodrama featuring can-can dancers raises funds to support civic activities.

Inside Passage Walking Tours

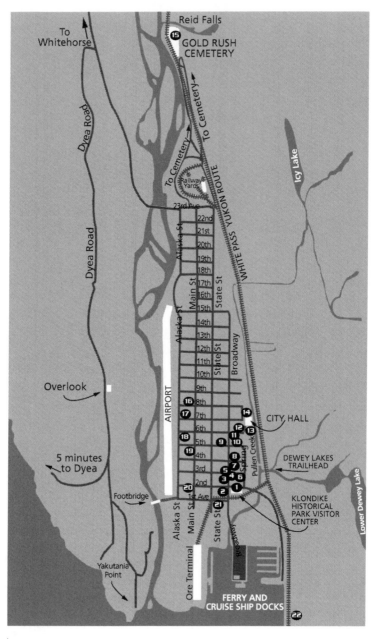

The Walking Tour

View down Broadway Street toward ship docks.

Skagway Walking Tour

Skagway is a compact, flat town that's great for walking. This tour takes you through the main shopping area and historic district. You'll see displays about gold rush history at both the Klondike Gold Rush National Historical Park visitor center and the Skagway Museum & Archives, the White Pass & Yukon Route, a monument to the "Angel of White Pass" and take a side trip to the Gold Rush Cemetery. Estimated time is 1 ½-2 hours, depending on stops, plus another 1 ½-2 hours round trip to the cemetery.

❶ This walking tour starts at the **Klondike National Historical Park Visitor Center** in the former White Pass & Yukon Route depot, a dark red building with yellow trim, on the corner of Broadway Street and Second Avenue.

From anywhere downtown, head down Broadway toward the waterfront. The park visitor center is to the left on the corner at Second Avenue.

From the ferry terminal or the cruise ship docks, head toward the center of the pier area and walk into town on Broadway. The park visitor center is to the right at Second Avenue.

Coming from the piers, you'll see a large information kiosk that will help orient you to downtown Skagway. You'll also see a large WP&YR snow plow, that once cleared the tracks in winter.

Inside Passage Walking Tours

Stop to Shop Most shops line Broadway and side streets in the central downtown area. A few suggested places to stop and shop:

Skaguay News Depot and Books, 264 Broadway. Its name hearkens back to an earlier spelling. Large collection of Alaska and Yukon titles, magazines, maps, postcards, children's books. Open all year.

Lynch & Kennedy Dry Goods, 352 Broadway. Native and locally made artworks, hand-painted T-shirts, custom jewelry, home accessories. Open all year.

Kirmse's Curios, Broadway and Fifth. Established in 1897. See Soapy Smith's pistol and the world's largest and smallest gold nugget watch chains. Gold nugget jewelry made here. Store only accepts cash. Seasonal.

Corrington's Alaskan Ivory, 525 Broadway. Combination shop/museum. Features scrimshaw walrus ivory, fossil mammoth ivory, baleen baskets, soapstone, bone and totem pole carvings. Seasonal.

Alaska Artworks, 555 Broadway. One-of-a-kind works, ranging from sterling silver, gold and fossil ivory artwork and jewelry to carvings, wildlife prints and watercolors. Seasonal.

The old red-and-yellow WP&YR depot (1898) and the adjacent yellow-and-green WP&YR railroad office building (1900) were used until 1969, when a new depot was built next door (that's where you catch the train today). The old depot now houses the national park visitors center, which offers a number of free programs during the summer: ranger-guided tours of the historic district; a 30-minute film, **Days of Adventure, Dreams of Gold**; and ranger talks on a variety of subjects (10 a.m. daily). Displays include a bronze plaque dedicated to the thousands of pack animals that died on White Pass during the Klondike Gold Rush; a representation of the "ton of goods" that each miner had to haul over the passes; a reproduction of the historic newspaper front page trumpeting the arrival of the first miners in Seattle; and enlargements of historic photographs of early-day Skagway and the stampeders. Information on hiking the Chilkoot Trail is available at the front desk. Open early May to late September, 8 a.m.-6 p.m. daily. For information, call 907-983-2921.

From the park visitors' center, turn left and cross Broadway to the second building from the corner.

❷ Jeff. Smiths Parlor was built in 1897 as Skagway's first bank. After arriving in 1897, the notorious outlaw Jefferson Randolph

"Soapy" Smith and his henchmen operated a saloon and gambling hall in this building. Originally located on Sixth Avenue at Broadway Street (where the Wells Fargo Bank now stands), it has been relocated twice and a couple of additions have been tacked on. However, the front still looks much as it did during the gold rush. Soapy was shot around the corner – there's a marker at First and State indicating the approximate location (Stop #21)

Inside Passage Walking Tours

Grabbing a Bite Following are a few suggested dining spots. The number indicates where to look for them along the walking tour.

Sweet Tooth Cafe, 315 Broadway (Stop #5). Located in a former saloon with its original marble bar and pressed tin ceiling. Casual local hangout. Homemade doughnuts, breads, soups. Train box lunches. Open daily all year. Breakfast, lunch. $

Corner Cafe, 4th & State St., (Stop #7) Where the locals lunch; off the main drag. Typical '50s American Diner: Hamburgers, sandwiches, soups. Friendly staff. Seasonal. Breakfast, lunch. Phone: 907-983-2155 $

Skagway Brewing Co., 700 Broadway (Stop #14). Upscale pub grub, fish & chips, salads, homemade desserts, micro brews (spruce tip ale, amber, hefeweizen and more). Bar open until 1 a.m. Phone: 907-983-2739 (983-BREW) $$

Stowaway Café, 205 Congress Way (Stop #22). Overlooking the marina. Alaskan food of Thai and French descent, Cajun style, seafood, steaks, decadent desserts. Open daily summer only, 4-10 p.m. Dinner. Reservations recommended; call 907-983-3463. $$-$$$

Skagway Fish Co., 210 Congress Way (Stop #22). Also overlooking the marina. Great for seafood, chowder, fish & chips. Open daily summer only, 11 a.m. to 11 p.m. Lunch, dinner. Reservations recommended; call 907-983-3474 (983-FISH). $$-$$$

↳ *Head back to Broadway, turn left and cross Second.*

❸ Broadway passes through the **main shopping area** and the heart of the six-block-long **historic district** – bounded roughly by Second and Seventh Avenues on the south and north, and by State and Spring Streets to the west and east. Most of the buildings in this district are original, constructed from 1897 to 1900. However, from 1900 to 1915 some were relocated to the central area when Skagway was shrinking in size after the gold rush.

On the northwest corner of Second and Broadway is the **Red Onion Saloon**. Built in 1898, it was a dance hall and saloon, with a brothel upstairs. On the back bar, a doll represented each "working girl." When she was with a client, the doll reclined; it was upright when she wasn't busy. The money paid upstairs – preferably in gold – was dropped through slots in the floor for safekeeping by the bartender. Mannequins peering from the upstairs windows give a sense of the days when the "girls" were in residence. The building also is reputed to have a ghost.

↳ *Proceed up Broadway half a block.*

You'll pass the former Washington Fruit Store (built in 1899 by the Rapuzzis, a pioneer Skagway family) and the 1900 building that originally housed the Washington & Alaska Steamship Co. office. A gift shop now occupies both buildings.

❹ Three doors up from the Red Onion is "the most-photographed building in Alaska," the **Arctic Brotherhood Hall.** Built in 1899, the AB Hall was the headquarters of a now-defunct secret fraternal organization. The Arctic Brotherhood was formed on board the steamship City of Seattle by 11 gold seekers. The Skagway group eventually numbered 300 and there were about thirty "camps" throughout Alaska and the Yukon, including Dawson City and Nome. The last person initiated into the Skagway AB camp was President Warren G. Harding in 1923.

The building's facade, considered a prime example of Victorian Rustic architecture, was made from 8,883 driftwood sticks

collected on the tide flats. AB member Charles O. Walker is credited with creating the facade in 1900 (it was restored in 2004-05 and the sticks counted). From across the street, you can see the driftwood letters "1899," "AB," and "Camp Skagway No. 1." The group's gold pan and nuggets insignia is at the top.

The AB Hall houses the **Skagway Visitor Information Center**, which is operated by the Skagway Convention and Visitors Bureau. Drop in and get the lowdown on what's happening and what to do in Skagway – they have loads of materials. Call 907-983-2854 for information. ⏀ ♿

⼈ Continue up the street to the corner of Third and Broadway.

The 1900 building you pass on the way originally was the Alaska Steamship Co. office.

❺ On the southwest corner of Third and Broadway is the three-story **Golden North Hotel**, now home to retail shops. The lobby has been remodeled and restored. This is Skagway's second Golden North Hotel. The original was located on Fourth Avenue, between State and Main Streets. The present building, with its distinctive

domed turret, was built a block away on the corner of Third and State Streets in 1898 as the two-story Klondike Trading Company. In 1908, George Dedman and Edward Foreman, owners of the first Golden North, bought the building, moved it, and added a third floor.

The building is reputed to have a gold rush-era ghost. Note for movie buffs: The wolf dream scene in the movie *Never Cry Wolf* was shot at the Golden North in 1981.

Across Third, look for the **Sweet Tooth Café**, 315 Broadway. ✗ SWEET TOOTH CAFE

♫♠ *Cross Broadway Street.*

❻ **The Mascot Block** – the three buildings at Third and Broadway – is owned by the National Park Service. All three have been repainted their original colors. **The Mascot Saloon** (1898) was one of some 70 saloons then operating in Skagway. Now part of Klondike Gold Rush National Historical Park, the building houses an excellent exhibit of an old-time saloon. 🏠 ♿

Next door is the 1898 building that formerly housed the Pacific Clipper Line, one of several steamship companies that had their offices in this part of town, and the former Hern Liquor Store, built in 1937.

Other gold-rush era buildings in this block include the Skaguay News Depot (1899), the Richter complex (three adjacent buildings constructed in 1899, 1929, and 1972) and the small building at the south end, now a liquor store but originally constructed in 1898 as the Hot Scotch Saloon. In the middle of the block is French Alley. The second building down the alley, now an office, is a 1902 "crib," a small building used by early-day prostitutes.

Inside Passage Walking Tours

ᴧᴧ *From the Mascot Block, proceed north on Broadway from Third to Fourth Avenue.*

Most of the buildings you'll pass on Broadway between Third and Fourth were built at the turn of the 20th century, including the Lynch & Kennedy building (1900).

Across the street, in the center of the block, is Dedman's Photo, built in 1897 as the studio for gold rush photographer E.A. Hegg. George Dedman arrived in 1898 with $16 and an iron in his suitcase. A "lady of the evening" allowed him to launder a pair of sheets, thus launching Dedman in the laundry business. He was one of the owners of the first Golden North Hotel and later purchased the building that houses the present Golden North. His wife established the photography business, which is still run by members of their family.

❼ On the corner of Fourth and Broadway is the tallest building in Skagway, the three-story **Pack Train Building**, constructed in 1904 as Army barracks and relocated from a site two blocks up Broadway. The corner business was a saloon called The Trail (the big sign on the Fourth Avenue side reading "U-AU-TO-NO-THE-TRAIL" dates from that time).

Who Struck it Rich?

It's estimated that 40,000 men and women went off in search of gold in the Klondike. Of that number, it's further estimated that only 20,000 actually looked for gold, 4,000 found gold, less than 100 became wealthy and only about 12 remained wealthy for life. Among the most successful of those who sought their fortune was Seattle's John Nordstrom, founder of the company known today as the Nordstrom Department Stores.

One block to the left across Broadway is the **Corner Café**, 4th & State St. Ⅴ CORNER CAFÉ

ᏔᏮᏡ Continue on Broadway across Fourth Avenue.

As you cross the street, look up on the bluff for the "**Kirmse's clock**," a large timepiece painted on the rock around the turn of the 20th century. Originally commissioned by jeweler Peter Kern, it was later maintained by another jeweler, Herman Kirmse, and his descendants.

8 Behind the Skagway Hardware store (1900), is the historic **St. James Hotel** (1898) – now used as a warehouse. The saloon of this hotel is where the deal was struck in the spring of 1898 to build the White Pass & Yukon Route. Local lore has it that Sir Thomas Tancrede, representing railroad investment interests in London, and Canadian Pacific Railway contractor Michael J. "Big Mike" Heney met by chance, talked through the night, and reached agreement by dawn.

Just down the street from the St. James are former **U.S. Army barracks from World War II**.

The trailhead for the **Dewey Lake trail system** is straight ahead across the railroad tracks.

ᏔᏮᏡ Return to Broadway and turn right toward Fifth Avenue.

9 Between Fourth and Fifth Avenues are buildings that date from the gold rush era.

Two doors up from the hardware store is the **Keelar the Money King Store** (1900). Frank Keelar was the self-described "Money

King of Alaska," a wheeler-dealer who advertised: "Loans Money-Buys Outfits." According to Keelar, he not only owned "mines, saw mills, steamboats, timber lands, and townsites," but also had "barrels of money." The building is now a liquor store.

ᑭᕋ Turn right on Fifth Avenue, go halfway down the block and cross the street.

🔟 On a large, grassy lot is the log **Moore Cabin**, built in 1887 as the residence of the founder of Skagway, Captain William "Billy" Moore. To the right is the house built in 1897 by Moore's son Bernard. To the left is the former Goldberg Cigar Store (1897). The buildings were restored by the National Park Service.

NPS archaeologists have discovered that the lawn between the cabin and the cigar store is the beginning of the historic White Pass Trail, one of two routes used by the stampeders to reach the Klondike.

ᑭᕋ Retrace your steps back on Fifth Avenue to Broadway, turn right and continue to Sixth Avenue.

Across Broadway is the **Corrington Museum of Alaskan History**, inside a gift shop at 525 Broadway

Between Fifth and Sixth Avenues, you'll pass the Kirmse Jewelry Store (1899) and two other gold rush-era buildings.

⓫ On the southeast corner of Sixth and Broadway is **Eagles Hall**, venue for Skagway's "Days of '98" show, Alaska's longest running theatrical production, dating to 1927. The hall comprises two 1898 hotels, the Mondamin and the Pacific, placed end-to-end in 1920. The show, a Gay '90s melodrama featuring "Soapy Smith" and a re-creation of the historic shootout, as well as dance hall girls, can-can dancing, and ragtime music, plays nightly during the summer season. Show times are posted at the theater, or call 907-983-2545 for information.

Diagonally across from the Eagles Hall is Wells Fargo Bank, with the only ATM in Skagway. Next to the bank is the U.S. Post Office. ▣ ✉

𝤮 *Turn right on Sixth. As you near the end of the block, cross the street.*

⓬ **Mollie Walsh Park** is dedicated to a young woman who arrived alone in Skagway in the fall of 1897 and came to be known as "The Angel of White Pass" for her kindness to the miners at a "grub tent" she operated on the White Pass Trail. Numerous packers vied for her attentions, most notably "Packer Jack" Newman, who shot and killed a rival in a fit of jealousy. After an argument with Newman about still another packer, Mollie married the other man, Mike Bartlett. The Bartletts eventually moved to Seattle, where Mike shot and killed Mollie in 1902 in a jealous rage. Newman was heartbroken when he learned of her death and in 1930, a year before his own death, he commissioned the bronze bust in this park. 🎁

Across from the park is the two-story former Peniel Mission (1900), now owned by the National Park Service.

⚡ From the park, continue to the right, around the corner to a path past the ruins of the Pullen House hotel on the right.

⓭ Harriet "Ma" Pullen left a bankrupt farm in Washington state and hit Skagway in September 1897 with just $7 and a few possessions. Working in a tent restaurant, she baked pies from dried apples. Later she opened her own restaurant and rented out rooms in her three-story house, eventually buying the building

Gold Rush Ghosts

Skagway is just the kind of place where you'd expect to see ghosts.

The most famous one is "Mary," who reputedly resides in Room 24 at the Golden North Hotel. Mary came to Skagway during the Klondike Gold Rush to wed her fiancé. Telling her to wait at the hotel, the young miner went off and was killed in the Palm Sunday avalanche on Chilkoot Pass. Refusing to believe he had died, Mary faithfully waited in her room, eventually dying of consumption. "She roams the halls in a long white gown, sometimes in a veil, sometimes with her hair piled on her head," said a former owner.

The Red Onion Saloon also claims a ghost, described – usually by men – as "a hostile female presence." There's a whiff of perfume when the "presence" is present, and she's credited with locking doors, making pounding noises upstairs (where the brothel used to be) and watering plants in the owner's locked office.

The Eagles Hall has a ghost, too. This one's a blond, blue-eyed boy ghost. "Any officer who's been doing the books late at night has felt its presence," claims one local.

and several others on the property. Her **Pullen House** became known as the finest hotel in the North. It operated for another decade after her death in 1947.

All that remains of the famous Pullen House is a tall stone chimney. The property is overgrown with trees and bushes, so it's not easy to photograph much of anything, including the chimney. (Please respect that the ruins are on private property and do not trespass.)

(↖ Continue along the dirt path, crossing a small footbridge over Pullen Creek.

In the creek you may see Dolly Varden trout and salmon spawning in the summer.

❿ The footpath leads to **City Hall** and the **Skagway Museum & Archives** (also known as the Trail of '98 Museum) at 7th Avenue & Spring Street in the McCabe College building, one of the few stone buildings in Alaska. Built of native granite in 1899 as a Methodist school, Alaska's first institution of higher learning closed due to financial difficulties. From 1901 to 1956, the building housed the U.S. District Court and U.S. Marshall's Office.

The museum showcases a fine collection of Alaska Native baskets, beadwork, and carvings; and a fascinating Gold Rush collection of memorabilia, artifacts and tools. Open daily May-Sept.: Mon.-Fri. 9 a.m.-5 p.m.; Sat.-Sun., 1-5 p.m. Oct.-April, call the museum for hours. Admission: Adults $2; students $1; children 12 and under free; group rates available. For information, call 907-983-2420.

Inside Passage Walking Tours

To the right on Spring Street from the McCabe building are:
- **Veterans Park and Gold Rush Diorama**, on the corner of 7th and Spring.
- The **Skagway Sculpture and Flower Garden**, between 7th and 8th avenues, a private collection of works by major sculptors in a peaceful garden, with an art shop/gallery. Open May-Sept. 9 a.m.-5 p.m. Admission: $7.50 for adults, children under 12 half price.

From the McCabe Building, go straight ahead (west) on Seventh Avenue to Broadway.

To the right is the **Skagway Brewing Co.**, 700 Broadway. Y SKAGWAY BREWING CO.

From 7th and Broadway, there are three options.

> ### They Call the Wind ... Skagway
>
> "Skagua" was the Tlingit name for the place. The name has various translations, most of which have something to do with wind. As Ben Moore, son of the city's founder, wrote: "Skagway is a name very typical of a place where the same air is never breathed twice."
>
> Skagway takes a direct hit both from the bone-chilling winds that whistle off the mountains to the north and those that scream up Lynn Canal from the south. "The wind sounds like a freight train coming down the valley," said a local. "There are far more windy days than calm days. In fact, when it is calm, you know something's different as soon as you step outside. It's quiet." Another noted that in 1938 the wind was so strong it blew over the train cars of the White Pass & Yukon Route.

OPTION A: To conclude your walking tour, turn left and return on Broadway – it's just five blocks back to the starting point.

OPTION B: Continue the walking tour to the Gold Rush Cemetery by proceeding on Seventh to State Street, then head out of town on a 30- to 45-minute walk to the cemetery.

OPTION C: Pass up the walk to the Gold Rush Cemetery, but continue the walking tour in town. Proceed on Seventh across Broadway, turn right on State Street to Eighth Avenue, turn left and proceed one block to Main Street (skip to Stop #16).

OPTION B:

To continue to the Gold Rush Cemetery, proceed straight ahead on Seventh across Broadway one block to State Street.

Seventh Avenue is the location of Skagway's former red light district. During the gold rush, prostitutes' "cribs" (small huts) lined the alleyways between Fourth and Seventh avenues. After the gold rush, they were moved to Seventh, most closing down by 1910.

Turn right on State Street and walk 16 blocks to 23rd Avenue. Continue to the left on 23rd for about two blocks.

From Seventh and State, it's about 1 ½ miles on level sidewalk or street to the Gold Rush Cemetery. The boardwalks of Skagway's historic district give way to concrete sidewalks that pass through a mostly contemporary residential area. On State Street you may see ore trucks with huge "pots" on the trailers, hauling lead and zinc ore from Yukon Territory mines to the terminal – the "biggest little ore house" – at Skagway's harbor.

You'll pass the WP&YR yards on the right. Look for brown and white park service signs directing the way to the cemetery. (You may be tempted to take a shortcut through the WP&YR yard, but this is private property and you could be cited for trespassing.)

ⵉⵣ Turn right off the main highway onto a road that loops around the WP&YR yards. Follow the road across the railroad tracks and continue about 0.4 mile (10 more minutes) to the cemetery on the right.

---

⑮ The **Gold Rush Cemetery** was Skagway's city cemetery during the gold rush and dozens of pioneers and stampeders are buried here. The cemetery was used from 1897 until 1908, when another site was developed across the Skagway River. Among the notable Skagwayans buried here are Frank Reid and Jefferson Randolph "Soapy" Smith, who killed each other during a shoot-out in 1898. There's a path up the hill a quarter mile to 300-foot-high Reid Falls.

You'll also see "the world's biggest gold nugget," a gold-painted boulder chained near the grave of Martin Itjen, an Austrian immigrant who was Skagway's first tourism promoter. Itjen was an early-day Skagway character; his Skagway Street Car Company conducted tours that included the cemetery. (The street car company has been revived and operates local tours with antique national park sightseeing cars.)

🚶 *Retrace your route back to town along the dirt road, 23rd Avenue and State Street to Eighth Avenue. Turn right on Eighth and proceed one block to Main Street.*

On the way, you'll pass by the **Skagway Public Library** on the southwest corner of Eighth and State.

⑯ At Eighth and Main, is the "plantation-style" **White House**, built in 1902 as the home of saloon owner and civic leader Lee Guthrie. Later the house was used as a hotel and was an Army hospital during World War II. It's now a bed-and-breakfast.

🚶 *Turn left on Main Street for one block, then turn right on Seventh Avenue for another block.*

⑰ Two historic houses are near the corner of Seventh Avenue and Alaska Street, on the right-hand side of the street.

The first you'll come to is the **Nye House**, which originated as a log cabin during the gold rush. Additions were made to it from 1898 to 1901. The house was the residence of Charley Nye, a power company executive.

The second house is the **Case-Mulvihill House**, a Victorian-style residence dating from 1904, when it was the home of W.H. Case, a partner in the noted photographic company of Case and Draper, who made many historic photographs during the gold rush. About 10 years later, William J. Mulvihill, chief dispatcher for the WP&YR, moved in with his family. (Mulvihill also was elected mayor of Skagway an astonishing 16 times.)

Inside Passage Walking Tours

At the corner of Seventh Avenue and Alaska Street, turn left for one block to Sixth Avenue, and turn left.

18 On the southeast corner is the **Gault House** (1899). This building may have originated as a saloon when Sixth Avenue was Skagway's primary business street. (The city was later re-oriented north and south and Broadway became the main business center.) For many years it was the home of Roy Gault, a WP&YR engineer.

Skagway's Big Mac Medivac

On Feb. 13, 1982, all of Skagway experienced a Big Mac attack of epic proportions.

The first McDonald's in Juneau had just opened and amid the fast-food frenzy occasioned by this event, the burghers of Skagway set about arranging a community order of burgers to be airlifted 95 miles northward. A local newspaper reported the feast included 200 orders of fries, 150 Big Macs and 50 Quarter Pounders. The community bill came to around $800 – about a dollar for every resident.

Nearly 200 people braved a wind chill factor of 40 below zero to await the arrival of the "Mac Attack Medivacs." After some initial freeze-up problems with their instruments, the school band serenaded the assemblage. Finally, 45 minutes late, two red cross-emblazoned Medivac planes rolled down the runway with a police escort, blue and red lights flashing. Wearing hospital greens, the pilots hustled the food into the terminal for distribution, while the band played "Old MacDonald Had a Farm."

Just what the doctor ordered to cure a bad case of cabin fever.

Continue on Sixth Avenue one block to Main Street and turn right one block.

19 Skagway's only remaining gold rush-era church is the **First Presbyterian Church**, on the southwest corner of Fifth Avenue and Main Street. The Methodists built it in 1901 after they sold McCabe College to the U.S. government. In 1917, a Presbyterian congregation bought it.

Continue down Main Street four blocks to First Avenue.

20 At the northwest corner of First and Main are **three houses built by the WP&YR** for its employees after the gold rush.

From First and Main, you can easily access a trail system to **Yakutania Point**, a picnic area overlooking the harbor, and secluded **Smuggler's Cove** – both less than a mile's walk. The trail to 4,900-foot **AB Mountain** also is in this direction. Continue south on Main Street for about two blocks, go around the airport terminal, cross a footbridge and turn left. It's well-marked and there are exercise stations along the way.

Turn left on First Avenue and return to Broadway Street and the dock area.

21 On the way, you'll pass a row of **mountain ash trees** planted along First Avenue. Plaques at the trees memorialize pioneer Skagway and Dyea families.

At First and State, you'll also pass the simple marker for the location of the July 8, 1898, **Frank Reid-Soapy Smith shootout** on the Juneau Co. wharf, which began

near this street corner and extended in the direction of the ferry terminal.

At Broadway, there are two options:

OPTION A: Conclude the walking tour by turning left to return to the National Park Service visitor center and the main shopping district, or right to the ferry terminal and cruise ship piers.

OPTION B: Continue the walking tour another 20-30 minutes to the marina, restaurants, Railroad Dock (Moore's Wharf), and the historic ship signature wall.

🏃 *Turn left on Broadway to 2ⁿᵈ Avenue, turn right and continue along second, which curves to the right and becomes Congress Way.*

On the right, you'll pass Pullen Pond. Chinook (king) and pink salmon spawn in the creek and pond in July and August.

American dippers may be seen along the creek year-round. Through the summer, look for rufous hummingbirds, northern goshawks, Townsend's warblers, kingfishers and other species. Winter birds include brown creepers and golden-crowned kinglets. Harbor seals, river otters, mink, marbled murrelets and pigeon guillemots may be seen from the waterfront.

🏃 *After about 10 minutes, you'll come to signs pointing left to restaurants and right to the waterfront promenade. Continue along the promenade.*

At right: "Soapy Smith's skull" and ship graffiti. Inset: waterfront promenade.

Overlooking the marina are:
- **Stowaway Café**, 205 Congress Way. ⅄ STOW-AWAY CAFÉ
- **Skagway Fish Co.**, 210 Congress Way. ⅄ SKAG-WAY FISH CO.

---

22 The waterfront promenade ends at the Railroad Dock (also known as Moore's Wharf, named for Skagway's founder). On the bluff overlooking the dock you'll see the **historic ship signature wall**. Since the early 20th century – possibly since the gold rush – the granite hillside has been the unofficial register of ships that have made maiden voyages to Skagway. Crew members recorded their ship's name, captain's name, company's logo and date of their visit. Access to the full length of the pier may be limited for security reasons. 📷

⋔ *Retrace your steps along the waterfront to Congress Way, 2ⁿᵈ Avenue and Broadway to conclude this walking tour.*

Inside Passage Walking Tours

Getting Out of Town

TAKE A HIKE: DEWEY LAKES TRAIL

The Dewey Lakes trail system is Skagway's most accessible. To reach the trailhead, walk east on Fourth Avenue toward the bluff, cross the footbridge over Pullen Creek and look for the sign on the other side of the railroad tracks.

It's a fairly easy 45-minute hike for slightly more than half a mile to Lower Dewey Lake, which is in the trees 500 feet above downtown Skagway. Upper Dewey Lake is approximately 2.5 miles beyond the lower lake, at 3,097 feet elevation, up a steep, strenuous, switchback trail through alpine country. The hike offers spectacular views of Skagway and the surrounding area. There is a trail shelter at Upper Dewey Lake.

Find Skagway-area trail maps at the Visitor Information Center, in the Arctic Brotherhood Hall, or the National Park Service visitor center, Second and Broadway.

WP&YR: RAILWAY BUILT OF GOLD

Alaska's first railroad, the White Pass & Yukon Route, was pushed through the rugged Coastal Mountain Range at the turn of the 20th century to provide stampeders easier access to the Klondike.

Construction of the 110-mile narrow-gauge railroad up White Pass from Skagway to Whitehorse, Yukon Territory, was an incredible engineering feat for its time. Completed in an astonishing 26 months, the railroad negotiates more than 500 curves along a roadbed hand-carved from sheer rock cliffs and passes through a 250-foot tunnel blasted through the rock. It climbs 2,885 feet from sea level in its first 21 miles. A major accomplishment in

Top photo at left: historic rail cars of the White Pass & Yukon Route. Clockwise from left center: artistic planter in Skagway yard; sculpture of Mollie Walsh; totem poles on Fifth Street boardwalk; "Kirmses Clock" painted on bluff; raconteur and businessman Steve Hites; lobby of Golden North Hotel; colorful Skagway business.

Inside Passage Walking Tours

1901 was the construction of a steel cantilever bridge arching 215 feet above Cutoff Canyon, at one time the highest railroad bridge in the world. The bridge has been replaced by a newer span, but the old one can be seen today from the passing train – particularly eerie on a foggy day when it looks like a ghost bridge to nowhere.

The railroad is designated an International Historic Civil Engineering Landmark. Excursions to the summit aboard the gold rush-era rail cars are sold on board cruise ships or at the WP&YR station, 231 Second Avenue (corner of Second & Spring). Call 907-983-2217 or 800-343-7373 for information.

Skagway's Still Soapy's Town

In some ways, Skagway is still Soapy Smith's town. The "Days of '98" show celebrates his nefarious feats. "Soapy," the actor, glad-hands visitors. Soapy's saloon still stands on Second Street (Stop #2). Although he operated for less than a year, Soapy Smith's legend lives on.

Jefferson Randolph "Soapy" Smith earned his con-artist reputation selling $1 bars of soap, some of which supposedly were wrapped in $5 to $50 bills. However, only his shills ever "won" a big bill. Arriving in lawless Skagway in the fall of 1897, Soapy and his gang established a saloon and gambling house, Jeff. Smiths Parlor [sic], and preyed on prospectors with various swindles, a protection racket and robbery. A notorious venture was his "Telegraph Office," which charged $5 (a significant sum in those days) to send a message. "Responses" arrived in a few hours, always collect. Business boomed, even though Skagway had no telegraph lines at the time.

Things came to a head on July 7, 1898, when miner John Douglas Stewart "lost" his $2,700 gold poke after two

Continued on next page...

CHILKOOT TRAIL: WORLD'S LONGEST MUSEUM

The 33-mile Chilkoot Trail was one of the major routes to the Klondike – and one of the most grueling. The last 4 miles – known as the Golden Stairs – is a strenuous 45-degree climb. During March and April of 1898, 1,200 to 1,500 steps carved in the ice provided access. Some of the most famous photographs of the gold rush were taken here, documenting the column of men and women struggling up the steep grade. Hazards abounded. The Palm Sunday avalanche on April 3, 1898, killed some 70 stampeders, many of whom are buried in the Slide Cemetery near the ghost town of Dyea. Today, the Chilkoot is known as the "world's longest museum," for the thousands of artifacts from the gold rush that line the trail (please do not touch or remove any artifact).

Skagway's Still Soapy's Town, continued

strangers encouraged him to leave it in a hotel safe overnight. Stewart complained loudly all over town, prompting the vigilante Committee of 101 (formed to squelch Smith) to demand the return of Stewart's money. Smith disavowed knowledge of the matter. The next night, a drunken and armed Smith appeared at a pier where the committee was meeting and challenged surveyor Frank Reid, one of four men standing guard. Shots were exchanged. Smith wounded Reid in the groin; Reid fired three shots, one through Smith's heart.

Smith died on the dock. Reid died 12 days later, acclaimed as Skagway's hero. Reid's grave at the Gold Rush Cemetery has an imposing granite monument. Nearby, adorned with a simple marker, is Smith's grave, just outside the cemetery boundary. Ironically, each July 8, Skagway commemorates the outlaw, not the hero, with "Soapy Smith's Wake," complete with champagne provided by Soapy's descendants.

Inside Passage Walking Tours

The route is just as rugged as ever. The weather can be cold and wet; you may have to hike through snow, even in July. A trail permit is required and you must pre-clear Canadian customs before you go. The trail attracts hikers from many countries. To manage demand for the route, prevent overuse and maintain the remoteness of trail, the National Park Service and Parks Canada have agreed upon a limit of 50 backpackers entering the trail each day. The trail is part of Klondike Gold Rush National Historical Park. For information, check with the park visitor center at Second and Broadway, or call 907-983-2921.

HOP OVER TO HAINES

Haines is just 15 miles by water down Lynn Canal from Skagway (360 miles if you drive), making it an easy day trip.

The Chilkat Bald Eagle Preserve near Haines is one of the best places in the world to see bald eagles. They flock to the Chilkat River each fall to feed on a late run of spawning salmon. The American Bald Eagle Foundation has an interpretive museum in Haines; free admission.

Other attractions are Fort William H. Seward, a National Historic Landmark, which offers a salmon bake and performances by the Chilkat Dancers; the Sheldon Museum and Cultural Center; and a re-created 1890s gold rush city.

An easy way to get to Haines is the Haines-Skagway Fast Ferry; phone 888-766-2103. Fares are: Adults: One way $35, round trip $68. Children (12 & under) half price. For other options, check with the Skagway Visitor Information Center in the AB Hall on Broadway; phone 907-983-2854.

U. S. Park Service replica of Russian blockhouse.

Sitka

Sitka at a Glance

Population:
   City and Borough of Sitka: 8,615 (24.7% Alaska Natives);
   51% Men; 49% Women; Visitors: 250,000 Annually

Geography:
   City and Borough of Sitka: 2,874 sq. mi. of land; 1,937.5
   sq. mi. of water Location: Sitka Sound on the west
   coast of Baranof Island fronting the Pacific Ocean, 95 air
   miles southwest of Juneau, 185 air miles northwest of
   Ketchikan and 862 miles northwest of Seattle.

Weather:
   Average summer temperatures: 48-61° F
   Average winter temperatures: 23-35° F
   Annual precipitation: 96"
   Solstices: Summer (June 21): almost 18 hours of daylight.
   Winter (Dec 21): 6 hours, 41 minutes of daylight.

Primary Industries:
   Fishing (551 residents hold commercial fishing permits),
   fish processing, tourism (104 cruise ship calls each
   summer), government, transportation, retail, healthcare
   services

Facilities and Services:
   A branch of the University of Alaska Southeast; Sitka
   Community Hospital and Mt. Edgecumbe Hospital (a
   regional medical center).
   Newspaper: Daily Sitka Sentinel.
   TV: KTNL TV-7 (CBS); cable and satellite service.
   Radio: KIFW-AM 1230; KCAW-FM 104.7 (public radio);
   KSBZ-FM 103.1 (Low-power FM radio station KAQU-LP
   88.1, owned by the city, broadcasts whale sounds from a
   submerged microphone at Whale Park.)

Visitor Information:
   Harrigan Centennial Hall Visitors Information Desk, 330
   Harbor Drive, 907-747-3225. Open during the summer.

   Sitka Convention and Visitors Bureau, 303 Lincoln Street,
   Ste. 4 (above Radio Shack downtown). Phone: 907-747-5940.
   Email: scvb@sitka.org

   Sitka National Historical Park Visitors Center, 106
   Metlakatla St., 907-747-6281. The nation's smallest
   national park.

Sitka

*Old records reveal that the Russians grumbled about the rain
when **they** were in the Sitka area, too.*

Sitka-by-the-Sea is a sparkling jewel in the necklace of port cities along the fabled Inside Passage. Its distinct personality is forged from Tlingit Indian roots and flavored by the Russian influence of the 18th and 19th centuries. Sitka pays homage to both cultures in restored Russian buildings and historic sites as well as a totem park and Native arts and crafts center. Downtown's major street diverges around Sitka's majestic centerpiece, St. Michael's Russian Orthodox Cathedral. When you walk through this charming town, you follow the still-echoing footsteps of an earlier era.

With a population of 8,600 and its location on the Pacific Ocean side of Baranof Island, Sitka has the small-town flavor (it got its first traffic light in 1992) and wilderness accessibility so prevalent in Southeast Alaska. It also hosts such cultural events as the Sitka Summer Music Festival, featuring world-renowned classical musicians; and Sitka Fine Arts Camp for youth. A branch of the University of Alaska Southeast lends its influence to the local milieu. But regardless of how high-falutin' the activity, Sitkans take it all in stride. A local noted that even for the music festival, "you can dress up or go in your XtraTufs (knee-high rubber boots)."

With mountains at its back and the Pacific at its doorstep, Sitka has a spectacular setting. And, its island life creates its own style. Garage sale-ing is very big, although as one local laughed: "Here we are on this rock and everything's just recycling from one house to another." A few independent folks prefer their own islands, residing on one of the dozen or so private islands in Sitka Sound and commuting via power- or rowboat.

This scenic site on Sitka Sound was occupied for hundreds of years by the Kiksadi Clan of Tlingits, who had four longhouses on what is now Castle Hill. The village was Shee-Atika, meaning "people on the outside of Shee (Baranof Island)." Shee-Atika provided a good life. The Tlingits harvested fish from the ocean, hunted deer and bear, and gathered berries. Their 60-foot-long cedar canoes journeyed north to the Copper River on the Gulf of Alaska and south to what is now Oregon and northern California.

"We have an inordinate amount of wildlife – a dozen or more whales spouting at any one time."

The year 1741 tolled the beginning of the end for this idyll. Vitus Bering, a Danish navigator in the service of the Russian czar, sailed east from Siberia's Kamchatka Peninsula. Those explorations led to the Russian colonization of Alaska, spurred by the hunt for sea otter pelts. Within a few years, 43 fur-trading companies were operating in Alaska; eventually the Russian empire extended from Fort Ross, near San Francisco, to the Aleutian Islands and even farther up the coast of the Bering Sea.

In 1799, Aleksandr Baranov, manager of the Russian-American Company, arrived at Shee-Atika. Wary of the Tlingits, Baranov built an outpost, Fort Archangel Saint Michael, at what is now called Old Sitka, 7 miles from downtown. The Kiksadis were equally wary of the Russians and in 1802 Chief Katlian and his warriors destroyed the fort. Baranov returned two years later with four ships and a contingent of Aleut warriors. The Kiksadis moved to a makeshift compound called Shish-Kee-Nu (meaning "Sapling Fort"), near the mouth of Indian River. The Russian ships opened fire, but the Tlingits remained quiet. A Russian landing party was launched and when it drew near Chief Katlian led a charge, wearing his Raven hat and brandishing a blacksmith's hammer acquired in the 1802 raid. The Russian and Aleut forces beat a retreat.

"If you want to get really wild, you have to go out of town – go to Juneau."

Six days of negotiations and bombardment continued, to no avail. During that time, the Tlingits' ammunition was inadvertently destroyed, leaving them in an untenable position. At dawn on October 7, the fort was eerily quiet. The Tlingits had slipped away in the night; the Battle of Alaska was over.

The Russians burned the compound and established a settlement called New Archangel, which became their new capital. The name "Sitka" – modified from Shee-Atika – came into use around 1847. During the 1800s it was the largest, most sophisticated city on the west coast of North America, hailed as the "Paris of the Pacific."

The Russian era concluded in 1867, with the United States' purchase of Russian America. New Archangel became Sitka and continued as the seat of government until 1906, when Juneau became the capital.

Inside Passage Walking Tours

A spate of gold mining, Sheldon Jackson Institute and the fishing industry sustained Sitka's economy. During World War

II, the town was fortified and the U.S. Navy built an air base on Japonski Island, which later became Mount Edgecumbe School, a boarding school for Alaska Native children. A large pulp mill operated from 1959 until 1993. Today, Sitka's economy depends on fishing, fish processing, tourism, government, transportation, retail and healthcare services.

Sitka's active arts community features several dance groups, numerous art galleries, two museums, and theater, music and choral groups. Sport fishing for salmon and halibut is popular, as are bird- and whale-watching. There are miles of trails and pathways for bicycling and walking or running.

FESTIVALS AND OTHER FUN

Special Sitka events include: the Sitka Jazz Festival in February; Sitka ArtiGras and Spring Gallery Walk in March; a week-long Mother's Day Quilt Show in May; Sitka Salmon Derby, with prizes for catching big fish, on Memorial Day weekend and the following weekend; in June, the three-week Sitka Summer Music Festival and the Sitka Fine Arts Camp for youth; the Running of the Boots fun run, late September, with prizes for the ugliest, biggest, etc. boots; Alaska Day Festival, with a week of events

One local laughed about Sitka's penchant for garage sales: "Here we are on this rock and everything's just recycling from one house to another."

leading up to the Oct. 18 reenactment of the transfer of Alaska to the United States; Native American Heritage Festival, month of November; Sitka WhaleFest in early November, with whale watching, workshops, art displays and more; and the Sitka Artisans Market, early December. Check the *Sitka Sentinel* to see what's going on when you're there.

DON'T MISS

- The Alaska Raptor Center (Stop #6 on the walking tour), where you can make the acquaintance of a bald eagle and other birds of prey.
- Sitka National Historical Park (Stop #7), to learn about Sitka's past and see Native artworks being created.
- The Russian Bishop's House (Stop #2), built for a prelate who held sway over an area extending from San Francisco to Japan.
- The views from Castle Hill (Stop #20), the best spot to photograph downtown, Sitka Sound and all around.
- St. Michael's Russian Orthodox Cathedral (Stop #11), with its priceless icons and other treasures.

Inside Passage Walking Tours

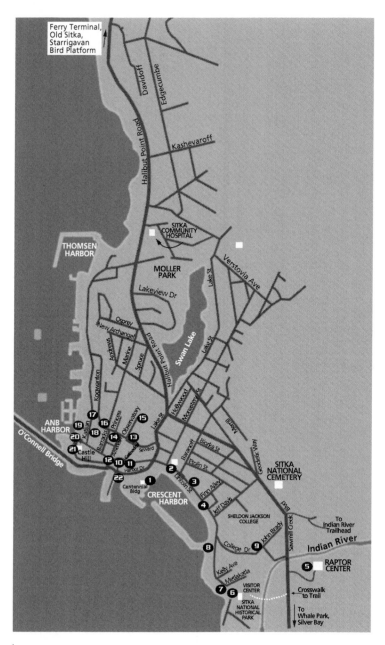

The Walking Tour

Hand-hewn Tlingit canoe at Centennial Hall.

Sitka Walking Tour

This walking tour takes you through Sitka's mostly level downtown. You'll see historic Russian buildings and a Native cultural center, learn about area history at Sitka National Historical Park and the Sheldon Jackson Museum, and have the option of seeing bald eagles face-to-beak at the Alaska Raptor Rehabilitation Center. The tour takes 2 to 2 ½ hours or more, depending on how long you linger at museums and shops. The walk to the Raptor Center adds at least another hour.

❶ The walking tour starts on the waterfront at the **Harrigan Centennial Hall Visitors Center**, 330 Harbor Drive.

> **🚶 If you're arriving at the cruise ship dock, it's to your left. If you arrive at the dock under the bridge, walk to your right on Harbor Drive for about 5 minutes. If you're coming from the ferry terminal, head into town on Halibut Point Road, turn right on Lake Street, which curves to the right to become Harbor Drive. Centennial Hall is to the left in the curve.**

Harrigan Centennial Hall was dedicated on Seward's Day, March 30, 1967, centennial of the United States purchase of Alaska from Russia. On the grounds is a large Tlingit canoe, hand-hewn from a single log. The building's brass door pulls copy Haida Indian argillite carvings of Raven and Bear. Find out what to see and do in and around Sitka at the information desk; 907-747-3225. 📱 ♿

Stop to Shop Numerous downtown shops offer everything from Alaska Native designs to Russian lacquer boxes and nesting dolls to smoked salmon and wild berry preserves. A few suggested places to shop:

Sitka Rose Gallery, 419 Lincoln St. Sculpture, painting, glass, woodturnings and Native art of more than 80 artisans from across Alaska.

The Russian American Company, upstairs in the MacDonald Bayview Trading Company, 407 Lincoln St. Russian lacquer boxes, icons, matryoshka (nesting) dolls, amber and Faberge jewelry, chess sets, samovars.

Fairweather Gallery and Gifts, 209 Lincoln St. Hand-painted clothing, original T-shirts and sweatshirts, silk scarves, jewelry, pottery and more.

Old Harbor Books, 201 Lincoln St. New and used books, nautical charts, maps, greeting cards. Books about Alaska, polar exploration and Russian-American history.

Made in Sitka Gift Shop, 200 Katlian St., in the Sheet'ka Kwaán Naa Kahidi Community House. Authentic, local Native artwork. Watch artisans demonstrate ancient art forms.

Absolute Fresh Seafood Inc., 475 Katlian St. Fresh, troll-caught wild Alaskan salmon, halibut, red snapper, spot prawns, king crab and smoked salmon. Custom processing for sport fishing. Nationwide shipping.

Centennial Hall houses the **Sitka Historical Museum**; 907-747-6455. The museum, which has a gift shop, provides an historical perspective for nearly everything you'll see in town. Displays include a scale model of the town as it looked in 1867, a Victorian parlor, Tlingit artifacts, a copy of the U.S. Treasury warrant used to buy Alaska, and Russian Orthodox icons. Hours: May-Sept., 9 a.m.-5 p.m. Sun.-Fri.; 11 a.m.-3 p.m. on Sat. Oct.-April, 10 a.m.-4 p.m., Tues.-Sat. Admission is $2. Special hours for school and Elderhostel groups and ferry stopovers. For additional information, call 907-747-6455.

This also is the summer home for the world-renowned **New Archangel Dancers**, who perform traditional Russian folk dances. Call 907-747-5516 for show times.

> **From Centennial Hall, walk out to Harbor Drive, then go right for about a block. Harbor Drive becomes Lake Street. Cross Lincoln Street and turn right (east) one block to Monastery Street.**

There's an ATM at First Bank, 203 Lake Street.

The **Bayview Restaurant** is upstairs at MacDonald's Bayview Trading Co., 407 Lincoln Street. BAYVIEW RESTAURANT

Lincoln Street follows the "Governor's Walk," so named because the Russian governor, Aleksandr Baranov, is said to have walked here often. You'll pass the **Hanlon-Osbakken House** (now Sitka Rose Gallery), built in the 1890s. A park along Lincoln Street borders **Crescent Harbor**, one of Sitka's four small boat harbors.

❷ On the corner of Lincoln and Monastery is the **Russian Bishop's House and Museum**, one of just four intact Russian buildings in North America. It was completed in 1843 and first occupied by Father Ivan Veniaminov – Bishop Innocent – whose diocese stretched from 60 miles north of San Francisco to 30

Inside Passage Walking Tours

Grabbing a Bite Following are a few suggested dining spots. The number indicates where to look for them as you follow the walking tour.

The Bayview Restaurant, 407 Lincoln St., #201. (Between Stops #1 and #2). Overlooking Crescent Harbor. Hamburgers, deli sandwiches, seafood, steaks, pasta, clam chowder and homemade desserts. Espresso, beer and wine. Open daily. Breakfast, lunch, dinner. $-$$

The Backdoor Cafe, 104 Barracks St. At the back of Old Harbor Books. (Stop #13). Cozy coffeehouse filled with local artwork. Custom roasted espresso, homemade bagels, pastries, pies and soups daily. Sooner or later, you'll meet everyone in town here. Breakfast, lunch. $

Ludvig's Bistro, 256 Katlian S. (Stop #17) Classy little bistro featuring tapas and "rustic Mediterranean fare." Open May-Sept., Mon-Sat 4-10 p.m. Dinner reservations advised; call 907-966-3663. $$-$$$

The Larkspur Café, 2 Lincoln St. (Stop #19) Menu features farmers' market produce and locally-caught seafood. Beer and wine. Live music some evenings; phone: 907-966-2326. Open Wed.-Sat. 11 a.m.-10 p.m., Sun. 10 a.m.-2 p.m. Closed Mon.-Tues. Lunch, dinner. $-$$

Van Winkle & Sons, 205 Harbor Dr. (upstairs). (Between Stops #21 and #22) Enjoy fresh seafood with a view of Sitka Sound. Lunch, dinner. Reservations advised; call 907-747-7652. $$-$$$

miles north of Hokkaido, Japan. The clergyman, teacher, physician and scientist spent 16 years at Sitka, his dedication earning him the highest ecclesiastical post in Russian Orthodoxy, Metropolitan of Moscow. He was declared Saint Innocent in 1977.

Listed on the National Register of Historic Places, the two-story building was built by Finnish shipwrights of logs with plank siding. The bishop's quarters and magnificent Chapel of the Annunciation are on the second floor; a school and orphanage

were on the first floor. The National Park Service acquired the building in 1972 and restored the building to its 1853 appearance over the next 16 years.

Open daily, 9 a.m.-5 p.m. during the summer. Admission is $4. Times of guided tours are posted. Winter hours by appointment. Call 907-747-6281.

The small building next to the Bishop's House was built c.1897 by the Orthodox Church and used as a school. In 1923, it became Sitka's first public library.

𝕃𝕄 Continue east on Lincoln Street for 1 ½ blocks, passing Baranof Street, the boundary of New Archangel in Russian times.

The home you'll pass on the northeast corner of Lincoln and Baranof Streets is the **Emmons House**. On the National Register, it was built in 1895 by U.S. Navy Lt. George Thornton Emmons, who wrote about the Tlingits for the Museum of Natural History in New York and became a leading Alaska anthropologist.

❸ At 611 Lincoln Street, Gothic-style **St. Peter's-by-the-Sea Episcopal Church** (one of the few stone buildings in Alaska) was built in 1899 under the auspices of Bishop Peter Trimble Rowe, Episcopal Bishop of Alaska. The congregation waited two years for their stained glass rose window. After it was installed, a con-

cerned parishioner pointed out to Rowe that they had probably received another church's window, since the small center design was a Star of David. Rowe reportedly admonished the parishioner: "Don't say anything. They'll never notice."

Rowe and members of his family are buried in the front yard. Behind the church is the See House, designed and built by the bishop in 1905, which houses church offices and a fellowship hall.

🏃 From St. Peter's, continue east on Lincoln.

On the left, you'll pass the **Moore House**, built in 1899. Across the street, the harbor park continues. Pavilions shelter benches and picnic tables.

🏃 Cross Lincoln and walk along the park for a short way.

4 Just before the tennis courts, there's a large flat rock – about 2 feet high and 5 feet long – known today as "Sitka's Blarney Stone." The "blarney" connection is unclear – possibly from an early-day promoter. But there are two other stories about this particular rock. One says it was "Baranov's Rock," because the Russian Governor used to rest on it during his constitutionals. According to earlier lore, the Tlingits called it "the Whetstone," because a long-ago chief sharpened his knives on it. 🎧

A short way farther, across from Sheldon Jackson College, is a larger rock with trees growing on it and a bronze plaque dedicated to the Rev. Dr. Sheldon Jackson. The Tlingit legend referred to it as the "Grindstone" because the same chief used to grind the heads of his enemies on this rock.

🚶 Cross Lincoln again to Jeff Davis Street.

Sitka is perhaps the only place in the world where Jeff Davis and Lincoln Streets intersect. But this Davis was not the head of the Confederacy. General Jefferson C. Davis was a Union officer who fought under General Oliver O. Howard in the Civil War and became the first governor of Alaska after the transfer in 1867.

At this point, there are two choices: Continue straight ahead to **Sitka National Historical Park** or take an optional route to see the **Alaska Raptor Center**, then visit the park.

🚶 To go to Sitka National Historical Park continue east on Lincoln past the campus of former Sheldon Jackson College for 5 to 10 minutes. (Skip to Stop #6)

OPTION: This route takes you to the Alaska Raptor Center, 1000 Raptor Way, and into Sitka National Historical Park the back way. It's about 20 minutes to the Raptor Center and another 15 to 20 minutes to the park visitor center, but the whole detour can take an hour or more, depending on how long you visit the Raptor Center.

🚶 From Lincoln Street, walk up Jeff Davis Street about four blocks to Sawmill Creek Boulevard, turn right, and follow the walkway/bike path on the right side of the road.

Across the highway is **Sitka National Cemetery**, one of the smallest national cemeteries in the United States. The oldest burial was in 1867. Just past the cemetery is the Alaska Public Safety Academy, where Alaska State Troopers are trained.

🏃 Cross the highway on the marked crosswalk in front of the academy and continue to the right for about 10 minutes. Look for the Raptor Center sign after the bridge over Indian River and walk up the hill for about 5 minutes to the Raptor Center.

❺ The **Alaska Raptor Center**, founded in 1980, is Alaska's primary facility for injured birds – from

hummingbirds to bald eagles. The center treats 100-200 birds each year, most injured through interaction with humans, releasing them after rehabilitation. Non-releasable eagles, owls and other raptors are placed in breeding programs or become educational birds. Photographs are permitted. The center is a nonprofit, volunteer-operated facility, with a bird clinic, classrooms, auditorium and gift shop.

Open 8 a.m.-4 p.m., May-Sept. Admission is $12 for adults, $6 for children 12 and under. Guided tours available May-Sept.; call 907-747-8662 or 1-800-643-9425 for information or to confirm hours.

🏃 Go back down the hill and continue to the left on the path for another 10 minutes, crossing the highway at the marked crosswalk and then

> *walking right to the park entrance, marked by park service signs. Follow the trail through the forested park for about 10 minutes, over the Indian River footbridge, to the visitor center.*

---

6 Sitka National Historical Park is Alaska's oldest and smallest national park, located on land set aside in 1890. It became a national historical park in 1972 and encompasses several sites significant in Sitka's Tlingit and Russian history, including the site of the Kiksadi Tlingit compound Shish-Kee-Nu ("Sapling Fort"); the 1804 battleground; the Russian Bishop's House; and the Russian blockhouse downtown. The center has an excellent exhibit of Alaska Native artifacts, including tools, baskets, jewelry, Tlingit house fronts and house posts. A movie about Sitka's past is shown in the auditorium.

One wing is devoted to the **Sitka Cultural Center**, which provides instruction in traditional arts, including carved wood, silver, weaving and beadwork. In the summer, at least one artisan usually is at work from 8 a.m. to 5 p.m.; questions and conversation are welcome.

A one-mile trail is lined with 11 totem poles, many carved in the 1930s as replicas of poles collected by Governor John Brady in the early 20th century and displayed at the St. Louis and Portland Expositions. The trail loops around the Kiksadi  fort site. Rangers conduct guided walks; check at the visitor center for times.

Summer hours: Daily, 8 a.m.-5 p.m. Winter hours: Mon.-Sat., 8 a.m.-5 p.m. The trail and park grounds are open 6 a.m.-10 p.m. in the summer; winter hours are shorter. Admission fees: May-

Inside Passage Walking Tours

Sept. $4 per adult; family pass $15. Children 15 and under, free. National Park passes honored. For more information, call 907-747-0110. 🕮 ♿

The New Archangel Dancers

Sitka's New Archangel Dancers, a troupe of about 30 women, performs 40 traditional dances from Russia, Belarus, Moldova and Ukraine. The performances are professionally choreographed and feature authentic costumes and music.

The group was formed in 1969 to promote Sitka's Russian history. Men were invited to join back then, but none would. Now, they're not allowed. (Sorry, guys.) The women perform all the roles, including male roles requiring great strength and endurance.

The all-volunteer, nonprofit group has performed all over the United States, as well as Japan, Canada, Mexico, Russia and other European countries. Well over a million people have seen their performances. During the summer, they perform up to five shows a day at Harrigan Centennial Hall on Sitka's central waterfront.

Admission is $10, with a portion of the proceeds going to a scholarship fund. A schedule is posted in Centennial Hall, or call 907-747-5516 for show times. Tickets are sold at Centennial Hall half an hour in advance of each performance. The New Archangel Dancers performance is included on city tours sold aboard many cruise ships or locally from Sitka Tours, 907-747-8443.

(⋔ From the visitor center, head out to Metlakatla Street, turn left back to town. Metlakatla turns into Lincoln Street at the corner.

7 Near the corner, to the left, a stairway leads down a short way to a scenic viewpoint and **Merrill Rock**. A plaque is dedicated to Elbridge W. Merrill, a photographer and the first custodian of the park, who lived in Sitka for more than 30 years. 📷

⋔ *Return to Lincoln Street and continue left 5 to 10 minutes.*

8 On the left is the **Sitka Sound Science Center**, 801 Lincoln Street, which offers the opportunity to experience the spectacular diversity of the many creatures that thrive in local waters. On display is a mural depicting Southeast Alaska's ecosystem and an 800-gallon Wall of Water exhibit. "Touch tanks" allow visitors to feel star fish, sea anemone and abalone. View four species of salmon in the non-profit hatchery. Visitors may take a self-guided tour of the grounds. Open 8 a.m.-5 p.m. daily. Suggested adult donation $2. For more information, call 907-747-8878.

⋔ *Cross Lincoln and walk up College Drive to the Sheldon Jackson Museum, the large octagonal building on the right.*

Arranged around a broad lawn are the buildings of the former **Sheldon Jackson College**. Before its closure in 2007, it was the oldest educational institution in Alaska, founded in 1879 and named for the famous Alaskan missionary and educator, the Rev. Dr. Sheldon Jackson. Author James Michener lived on the grounds for several months between 1984 and 1986 while researching his best-selling novel *Alaska*.

9 **Sheldon Jackson Museum**, 104 College Drive, was the first concrete building in Alaska. As the first general agent of education for Alaska, Sheldon Jackson traveled throughout the territory, acquiring an extensive collection of artifacts. In 1890, he built a museum, which was soon outgrown and replaced in 1895 with the current structure. In 1984, it became part of the state museum system.

The building provides a circular setting for the cases – original to the museum – displaying the artifacts, most pre-dating the 1930s and many collected by Jackson from 1888 to 1898. Tall cases line the perimeter, while cases of drawers are in the center. (Each drawer is a small adventure. You'll find ivory carvings, beadwork and fishing gear, among other intriguing items.) The collection represents Alaska's four major Native groups: Eskimo, Athabaskan, Aleut and Northwest Coast (including Tlingit, Haida and Tsimshian). Summer months offer a Native artist demonstration daily.

Open daily 9 a.m.-5 p.m., mid-May to mid-Sept. Winter hours: 10 a.m.-4 p.m. Tues.-Sat. Closed holidays. Admission is $4; children 18 and under, free. Call the museum at 907-747-8981 for more information or to make arrangements for visitors with special needs. Volunteers and staff are on hand to answer questions. A gift shop features Alaska Native handicrafts. 🚻 ♿

{\bf From the museum, walk back down College Drive to Lincoln Street, turn right and proceed the five blocks back to Lake Street. Cross Lake Street and continue on Lincoln to the cathedral.}

A **postal substation** is located at 338 Lincoln St.

⑩ Sitka's centerpiece is **St. Michael's Russian Orthodox Cathedral**, its onion dome and conical cupola visible from all over town. Its cornerstone was laid in 1844 and the original cathedral consecrated by Bishop Innocent on Nov. 20, 1848. The present-day building is an exact replica of the original, which burned on Jan. 2, 1966, in a fire that destroyed the central business district. The night of the fire, as the building burned around them, heroic Sitkans risked their lives forming a human chain to hand

the valuable treasures out of the building. Most moveable objects were saved, including the heavy entry doors and priceless icons – some dating to the 14th century. The original bronze bells, cast in Sitka's Russian foundry, were among the items lost.

Using the original blueprints, a fire-resistant cathedral was reconstructed over the next 10 years. New bells were cast from the melted remains of the originals and today all the rescued treasures are back in their original places. On the National Register of Historic Places, St. Michael's is an active church and the seat of the Russian Orthodox Church in Alaska.

Summer hours: 9 a.m.-4 p.m., unless otherwise posted on the door. Sundays by appointment only. For winter hours, call 907-747-8120. $2 donation requested.

🚶‍♂️ After exiting the front door of the cathedral, walk to the left across Lincoln Street to the Lutheran Church.

Near the cathedral are two banks with ATMs.

Inside Passage Walking Tours

⓫ **Sitka Lutheran Church**, 224 Lincoln Street, is the third church on this site, which was never in the possession of the United States, being deeded directly to the congregation by the Russians. The first church, built in 1841-43, was torn down in 1888. In 1940, a new congregation built another church – which burned in the 1966 fire. The present church was built in 1967. Mid-May to mid-Sept., volunteers lead free tours on which visitors can see artifacts from the first church, including the 1844 Kessler organ, chandelier, pulpit and communion rail.

🚶 Continue to the right (west) on Lincoln Street.

⓬ At 202/206 Lincoln Street is "**Building 29,**" one of only two Russian-American Company buildings remaining in Sitka and so-named because that was its number on the map drawn up to

"Paris of the Pacific"

During the 1800s, Sitka was the largest city on the west coast of North America. It became known as the "Paris of the Pacific" for its commercial, social and cultural activities. Splendid parties took place at the governor's home on Castle Hill. There was a tea garden and a race course. Ships of many nations called here. Furs were the main export to European and Asian markets, but fish, lumber and ice also were exported to Hawaii, Mexico and California. (Ice from shallow Swan Lake – packed in sawdust from the local sawmill – sold in San Francisco in the 1850s for $7 a ton, less 20 percent for melting.) The Russian shipyard built and repaired vessels and their foundry produced the bells not only for Sitka's original St. Michael's Cathedral, but also for numerous Spanish missions along the Camino Real Trail in California.

inventory Sitka's assets during the transfer from Russia. Building 29 was constructed in about 1835 to house employees of the Russian-American Company. Notice the "new" addition on the right-hand side of the building, constructed in 1884. A National Historic Landmark, the building is considered the finest remaining example of Russian secular architecture in Alaska.

The **Backdoor Cafe** is in the back of Old Harbor Books, across the way at 201 Lincoln Street. **Y** BACKDOOR CAFE

↟↟ From Building 29, cross Lincoln Street, turn right and continue past the cathedral to Cathedral Way. Turn left on Cathedral a block to Seward Street and turn left (west).

⓭ At Cathedral Way and Seward Street is **Rose Hill Place** (315 Seward Street). This Colonial Revival-style house, listed on the National Register, was built in 1911 as the home of Miss Mae Mills, sister of early-day Sitka merchant and banker W.P. Mills. Miss Mills used her large house as a home for orphans. She planted the large Balm of Gilead tree in the front yard.

↟↟ Continue west on Seward Street one block to Observatory Street.

⓮ On the hill at Seward and Observatory Streets is a large white house with a gambrel roof. On the National Register and now known as the **Forest Service House**, it was built in 1916 by the U.S. Department

of Commerce, Coast & Geodetic Survey, as offices and living quarters for the staff in charge of the seismological and geo-magnetic observatory. It now houses Tongass National Forest personnel. Prior to 1867, this was the site of the Russian Tea Garden.

↟↟ *Turn right on Observatory Street for about 2 blocks.*

15 At the north end of Observatory Street is the entrance to the **Russian Orthodox Cemetery**, with about 1,600 graves dating back to 1848, some marked with headstones made from the ballast of Russian ships. There has been an ongoing effort to restore the older areas and it is a peaceful place of quiet beauty which is still in use today. Please visit the cemetery with respect and preserve its history and dignity.

Happy Landings

Flying into Sitka can be a thrilling experience, especially if it's your first time. The 6,500-foot runway is about three-quarters surrounded by water, so it's like landing on a really large aircraft carrier. You always seem to find yourself wondering if the plane is going to stop before it runs out of pavement. (It does.)

Prior to the opening of the airport in 1967, and the O'Connell Bridge (the first cable-stayed, girder-span bridge in the United States) in 1972, Sitkans flew between their island city and Juneau aboard amphibious PBY Catalinas or float-equipped aircraft – and were ferried between downtown Sitka and Japonski Island aboard small shore boats.

🚶 *Return to Seward Street, turn right and continue for a few blocks to Marine Street, passing American, Princess and Barracks streets.*

OPTION: Turn up Princess Way for half a block. To the left, in the tiny Lutheran Cemetery, is the grave of Princess Adelaide Ivanovna Maksoutoff, who died in 1862. She was the first wife of Prince Dimitrii Maksoutoff, last of the 14 Russian governors of New Archangel. Buried next to the princess is Edvard Etholen, infant son of 1840s Governor Arvid Adolf Etholen and his wife Margaretha.

🚶 *Return to Seward Street and turn right.*

🚶 *At Seward and Marine, go up some steps and a path to the Russian Blockhouse.*

16 The **Russian Blockhouse** is a replica of those which stood along a Russian stockade built after the Battle of Alaska in 1804. The stockade was torn down in 1877 and the original blockhouses razed in the early 1900s. The U.S. Park Service built the replica in 1958; it is not open to the public. To the right, just above the blockhouse, is part of the old **Russian Orthodox cemetery**. There are good views of Sitka Sound and the O'Connell Bridge from the blockhouse area. 📷

🚶 *Retrace your steps back down the hill and turn right onto Kaagwaantaan Street for 1 minute, then to the left down a path and steps to Katlian Street.*

17 At the bottom of the steps is the **Sheet'ka Kwaan Naa Ka-hidi Tribal Community House**, 200 Katlian St. The community house offers dance performances, story telling, cultural events, a

gift shop featuring Native artwork and the largest hand-carved house screen ("Lovebirds") in Southeast Alaska.

The 30-minute **Naa Kahidi Dance Show** is an authentic Tlingit performance in a traditional-style clan house. Dancers in regalia sing ancient songs handed down through generations. Admission: Adults, $8; children, $5. For further information, contact the Sitka Tribe of Alaska at 907-747-7290 or 888-270-8687 toll-free or email: reservations@sitkatribe.org Website: www.sitkatours. com

About a block farther on the left-hand side of Katlian Street is the **Alaska Native Brotherhood Hall**, 235 Katlian Street. On the National Register of Historic Places, the ANB Hall was built in 1914 for the Alaska Native Brotherhood, founded in Sitka in 1912 to fight discrimination against Alaska Natives. Today, the ANB and the Alaska Native Sisterhood remain influential in preserving Native culture.

A short way past the ANB Hall is **Ludvig's Bistro**, 256 Katlian S. **Y** LUDVIG'S BISTRO

Retrace your steps back on Katlian past the Tribal Community House to the Pioneers' Home.

18 The **Sitka Pioneers' Home**, 120 Katlian St., dominates the western waterfront. The home originated as a log barracks built by the Russians in the 1800s; its grounds are on the site of the Russian parade ground. When the first Territorial Legislature

convened in 1913, it first gave women the right to vote, then established this Pioneers' Home as a haven for aging prospectors. Today the state operates several such homes statewide. This yellow stucco building with red tile roof was constructed in 1934; a women's wing was added in 1956. The home has about 75 residents. Visitors are welcome. On the first floor, a gift shop sells handicrafts made by the residents.

The 13 ½ -foot-tall clay and bronze statue is "The Prospector." Sculptor Alonzo Victor Lewis modeled it on a real pioneer, William "Skagway Bill" Fonda. Dedicated to the thousands of prospectors who pioneered Alaska, the statue was unveiled on Alaska Day, Oct. 18, 1949. (Look closely at the sculpture for details, such as the names of gold rush locales carved into the rifle butt.)

The Pioneers' Home is a great place to see **Sitka roses**. Introduced in 1902, the Rugosa or Turkestan roses (*Rosa rugosa*) are found all over town, but are especially bountiful here. The hedge blooms through the summer; from late September you'll see red rose hips.

From the Pioneers' Home, cross Katlian Street to Totem Square.

⓲ Katlian Street, bordering **Totem Square**, is on the site of the Russian shipyard. Totem Square was filled in during 1940-41 as a Works Progress Administration (WPA) project. In addition to the central totem pole displaying the double-headed eagle of Sitka's Russian heritage, there are a Russian cannon and three huge anchors believed to have been lost in Sitka Harbor from British or American ships in the 1700s

Inside Passage Walking Tours

🚶 *From Totem Square, head south across Lincoln and turn right for half a block to the corner.*

You'll pass the former Post Office and U.S. Courthouse Building, which now houses the offices of the City & Borough of Sitka.

20 Across the street, to the left, is the **Sitka Cable House**, 2 Lincoln St., built in 1909 for the Washington-Alaska Military Cable and Telegraph System (WAMCATS). WAMCATS was an overland and submarine cable telegraph system linking scattered military posts in Alaska with the Lower 48. Built from 1900-04, the cable operated until 1931, when a network of radio stations took over.

Upstairs is **Raven Radio** (KCAW-FM 104.7), a community/public station.

The **Larkspur Café** is on the first floor. **Y** LARKSPUR CAFE

🚶 *Retrace your steps back up Lincoln. A sign points the way to Castle Hill on a path to the right between the drugstore and the municipal building. Walk up the 78 steps.* 📷

21 **Castle Hill**, a 60-foot-high rock outcropping, is the oldest state park in Alaska and a National Historic Landmark. Before the Russians arrived in 1799, the hill, known as Noow Tlein (meaning "big fort"), was occupied by the four main houses of the Kiksadi Tlingits. After the 1804 battle, Russian Governor Aleksandr Baranov built the first of four residences that stood on this hill during the Russian period. The last one, built in 1836-37, was called Baranov's Castle (although he had left 18 years before) and was the center of social life. Later used for U.S. government offices, it burned in 1894.

Castle Hill is the site of Alaska's transfer from Russia to the United States on Oct. 18, 1867, and where the first 49-star American flag was raised on July 4, 1959, to honor Alaska statehood. On the perimeter are two cannon bearing the double eagle insignia of Imperial Russia. A plaque depicts Baranov's Castle at the time of the transfer.

The hill affords panoramic views of downtown Sitka, Sitka Sound, cruise ships and the O'Connell Bridge, a 1,225-foot span linking Sitka and Japonski Island, site of the airport. Across the sound on Rockwell Island is a white-and-red lighthouse, possibly the most-photographed home in Sitka. Not an official lighthouse, the private residence and B&B was built in 1985. Its light marks a reef 100 yards offshore. 📷

🚶 Descend Castle Hill via the trail down the side facing the sound. The trail splits at the bottom. To return to Lincoln Street, veer left through an alley. To continue the walking tour, turn right to Harbor Drive, then turn left. Cross Harbor Drive and continue left for about a block and a half to the library.

In the retail area on the left side of the street is **Van Winkle & Sons**, 205 Harbor Drive (upstairs). 🍴 VAN WINKLE & SONS

On the way, you'll cross Maksoutoff Street. To the right, the street ends on a 400-foot causeway to a little island. At the very end, #1 Maksoutoff Street, a private residence listed on the National Register of Historic Places, was built by merchant and banker W.P. Mills in 1915 on the foundation of a former Russian fish saltery.

The "Eruption" of Mount Edgecumbe

Rising 3,271 feet out of the Pacific Ocean about 15 miles west of Sitka, Mount Edgecumbe is one of the area's most eye-catching features. Beautiful and Fuji-like, the dormant volcano sat quietly for centuries. Then, on April 1, 1974, Oliver J. "Porky" Bickar, a member of Sitka's practical-joke-playing "Dirty Dozen," set about staging an "eruption."

"I got a hundred or so tires together," Porky recalled. "I woke up April Fool's Day and you could see the mountain so clear. You could see a thousand miles. I said, 'I'm gonna do it.'"

Porky began dialing for helicopter pilots. "I finally got ahold of Earl Walker, with Temsco in Petersburg over on the other side of the island. He was sitting there all fogged in. And he said: 'If I can see one more telephone pole, I'll come over.' And about an hour later, here he comes."

The pair flew over to the volcano with half the tires, plus some oily rags, gasoline and a few smoke bombs for good measure. "I placed them in the middle of the crater. Then I stomped 40- or 50-foot-long letters in the snow saying 'April Fools!'" Porky added black paint to highlight the letters. Earl returned with the rest of the tires and they set the whole mess on fire.

"We flew back real low and inconspicuous like," Porky chortled.

Black smoke billowed from Mount Edgecumbe's cone. The Coast Guard got all excited. Someone called an admiral and aircraft flew over for a look. Then came the radio message: "Looks like you've been had."

22 Kettleson Memorial Library, 320 Harbor Drive, was dedicated on Oct. 18, 1967, the centennial of the Russian transfer of Alaska. It was partially funded by and named for Theodore Kettleson, who managed the Pioneers' Home and co-founded the First Bank of Sitka.

The library has a collection of books about Alaska and Pacific Northwest Indians. Open Mon.-Fri. 10 a.m.-9 p.m.; Sat.-Sun. 1-9 p.m. Closed city holidays. Call 907-747-8708 for information. 🚻 ♿

From the library, walk back to Harbor Drive and turn right to return to Centennial Hall and the end of this walking tour.

Come in and Taste

Authentic
Russian Tea
from our Samovar

Inside Passage Walking Tours

Getting Out of Town

TAKE A HIKE: GAVAN HILL TRAIL

This popular trail is easily accessible from downtown Sitka. Just walk east on Lincoln to Baranof Street and follow Baranof about eight blocks to the end. The trailhead sign is just past the house at 508 Baranof Street.

It's 3.5 miles to the summit of Gavan Hill, but it'll take you 3 to 4 hours going up because of the fairly strenuous 2,500-foot elevation gain. The planked, stair-stepped trail provides good access to alpine country and offers excellent views of Sitka and its surrounding area. There's a hut at the summit for shelter.

TAKE A HIKE: INDIAN RIVER TRAIL

This trail also is popular and easily accessible from downtown. Head north on any street – Lake, Monastery, Baranof, Jeff Davis – to Sawmill Creek Boulevard and turn right. Walk 10 to 15 minutes and turn left on Indian River Road – it's the next road past the Alaska Public Safety Academy. Follow this road about half a mile to its end at a pump house behind a locked gate. If you drive, there's parking outside the gate. The trailhead is just to the left of the pump house.

This is an easy walk through the rain forest. (Remember, the operative word here is "rain," so be prepared for wet and muddy conditions.) The trail is 4.5 miles long, and the estimated one-way time to the 70-foot waterfall at the end is 1.5-4 hours. The trail climbs very gradually, for an elevation gain of 700 feet.

The trail up a wide valley offers magnificent views of the surrounding mountains. There are numerous picnic spots. Bears may

At left top: Ludvig's Bistro, Princess Maksoutoff's grave, plaque on Merrill Rock; Sitka Rose Gallery. At left center: totem in Sitka National Historical Park; Crescent Harbor; tribal resource center; Rockwell Island lighthouse. At left bottom: Castle Hill.

be present, particularly when salmon are spawning. But you may see other animals – maybe a deer – and birds.

FOR THE BIRDS: ST. LAZARIA ISLAND

The breeding grounds for thousands of seabirds, 65-acre St. Lazaria Island National Wildlife Refuge is located about 15 miles from Sitka as the puffin flies. In addition to tufted puffins, visitors will see rhinoceros auklets, murres, ancient murrelets, storm petrels, cormorants and numerous other birds, including bald eagles. The surrounding waters are home to humpback whales, sea otters, sea lions and harbor seals. The volcanic island was designated a wildlife refuge in 1909 and became part of the Alaska Maritime National Wildlife Refuge in 1980.

The birds and wildlife are best viewed from a boat. It takes approximately 45 minutes to an hour to reach the island from Sitka, depending on weather and sea conditions (take precautions if you're prone to motion sickness). Several tour companies operate excursions to St. Lazaria, including Alaska Wildlife Tours and Charters, 907-738-1062, and Sitka's Secrets, 907-747-5089. For other tour options, check with the Centennial Building Visitors Information Desk, 330 Harbor Drive, 907-747-3225 or Sitka Convention and Visitors Bureau, 303 Lincoln Street, 907-747-5940; website: www.sitka.org/tours.

Pie in the Sky

If you fly into – or out of – Sitka, be sure to drop by the Nugget Restaurant in the airport terminal for a slice of their renowned pie – they'll pack it "to go." Southeasterners in the know do just that on Sitka stopovers, returning to the plane with their boxes of fruit-filled or cream pie. There's just enough time to savor a slice of "pie in the sky" before the plane gets to Juneau.

FOR THE BIRDS: STARRIGAVAN PLATFORM

The Starrigavan Bird Viewing Platform is located in the Starriga-van Recreation Area near the end of Halibut Point Road, 7 miles north of Sitka (¾ mile past the Alaska Marine Highway ferry terminal).

A 500-foot boardwalk and interpretive trail provides access to a hemlock and spruce forest and wetlands for viewing spawning salmon, as well as waterfowl such as great blue heron, kingfishers, loons, scoters, harlequin ducks and mergansers.

A WHALE OF A GOOD TIME

Sitka has some of the best humpback whale watching in the world and Whale Park, located on a cliff about 6 miles south of town on Sawmill Creek Road, provides an opportunity to view them, as well as Steller sea lions and other marine mammals. They congregate in Sitka's waters in the early fall and winter to feed on herring.

Sculptures of cavorting whales greet you at the entrance and the park offers a sheltered picnic pavilion, viewing scopes, boardwalks and a stairway to the beach. (Listen to whale sounds on the city's low-power FM radio station KAQU-LP 88.1, which broadcasts from a microphone submerged at Whale Park.)

Whales also may be seen on marine wildlife tours available from several companies, including Allen Marine Tours, 907-747-8100 or 1-888-747-8101, or Alaska Outdoor Tours, 907-747-7266. For other tour options, check with the Centennial Building Visitors Information Desk, 330 Harbor Drive, 907-747-3225 or Sitka Convention and Visitors Bureau, 303 Lincoln Street, 907-747-5940; website: www.sitka.org/tours.

Inside Passage Walking Tours

ABOUT THE AUTHOR

A native of Seattle, author Julianne Chase Patton grew up in the Great Land, where she lived in nearly every region of the state, spending the longest time in Southeast Alaska, her favorite region. A graduate of the University of Alaska, Fairbanks, she worked as a newspaper reporter and editor for more than 14 years. In addition to being the author of *Inside Passage Walking Tours*, she wrote and edited two other travel guides, the first edition of the *Alaska Wilderness Milepost* and *Backcountry Alaska*, a travel book in the Alaska Geographic series. Juli visited Alaska regularly while working for one of the world's largest cruise lines. She and her husband Kevin live in the Puget Sound region of Washington State.

41712188R00089

Made in the USA
Columbia, SC
16 December 2018